The Apostate Angel

The Apostate Angel

A CRITICAL STUDY
OF GORE VIDAL

Bernard F. Dick

Random House   New York

All rights reserved under International and Pan-American Copyright
Conventions. Published in the United States by Random House, Inc.,
New York, and simultaneously in Canada by Random House of Canada
Limited, Toronto.

Library of Congress Cataloging in Publication Data

Dick, Bernard F.
    The apostate angel.

    Bibliography: p.
    1. Vidal, Gore, 1925–   —Criticism and Inter-
pretation   I. Title.
PS3543.I26Z65   818'.5'409   73-20553
ISBN 0-394-48108-9

Manufactured in the United States of America

9 8 7 6 5 4 3 2

First Edition

    For permission to quote, I would like to express my gratitude to the
following:
    E. P. Dutton and Co., Inc., for *In a Yellow Wood* (Copyright 1947 by Gore
Vidal); *The Season of Comfort* (Copyright 1949 by Gore Vidal); *A Search for the
King* (Copyright 1950 by Gore Vidal); *Dark Green, Bright Red* (Copyright 1950
by E. P. Dutton and Co., Inc.); *The City and the Pillar Revised* (Copyright ©
1965 by E. P. Dutton and Co., Inc.).

    Harcourt Brace Jovanovich, Inc., for *The Diary of Anaïs Nin: Volume Four
1944–1947* (Copyright © 1971 by Anaïs Nin).

    Holt, Rinehart and Winston, Inc., for *Screening the Sexes* (Copyright © 1972
by Parker Tyler).

    Little, Brown and Co., Inc., for *The Judgment of Paris* (Copyright 1952 by
Gore Vidal); *Messiah* (Copyright 1954 by E. P. Dutton and Co., Inc.; copyright © 1965 by Gore Vidal); *Visit to a Small Planet* (Copyright © 1956, 1957
by Gore Vidal); *The Best Man* (Copyright © 1960 by Gore Vidal); *Julian*
(Copyright © 1962 and 1964 by Gore Vidal); *Washington, D.C.* (Copyright
© 1967 by Gore Vidal); *Myra Breckinridge* (Copyright © 1968 by Gore Vidal);
Two Sisters (Copyright © 1970 by Gore Vidal).

    New Directions Publishing Corporation for Jean Paul Sartre, *Nausea*, trans-
lated by Lloyd Alexander (Copyright © 1964 by New Directions Publishing
Corporation. All rights reserved).

Acknowledgments

I must thank Gore Vidal for granting me so many interviews at a time when he was preoccupied with the Broadway production of *An Evening with Richard Nixon and . . .* , as well as for giving me the right to use and quote from his unpublished works; Jason Epstein and Cordelia Jason of Random House; Dr. Josephine L. Harper, manuscripts curator, and Miss Katherine Thompson, reference assistant, at The State Historical Society of Wisconsin at Madison, where the Vidal Papers are housed; Mr. Stanley B. Sofield, Vidal's former teacher at St. Alban's School; my colleagues Gene A. Barnett, Vartkis Kinoian, Benjamin Nelson, and Vernon L. Schonert; Professor Marilyn Weigold, and Ruth Schwartz, periodicals librarian at Fairleigh Dickinson University (Teaneck Campus). My greatest debt appears in the dedication.

For Katherine

So spake the apostate Angel, though in pain,
Vaunting aloud, but racked with deep despair.
—Milton, *Paradise Lost*

Contents

The Apostate Angel

Introduction

RECENTLY I PUBLISHED a study of Mary Renault's fiction in Southern Illinois University Press's "Crosscurrents/ Modern Critiques" series. Each book in that series contains a preface by the general editor, the ubiquitous Harry T. Moore. Since the preface takes the form of a short essay-review, the author never sees it until the book appears—a dubious practice, but understandable in an age of few surprises. The preface to my book began with a mild criticism of a review of John Hersey's *The Conspiracy* that had appeared in a "national magazine." Professor Moore noted that the "young" (bless him!) reviewer compared Hersey's novel about Neronian Rome with historical fiction by Robert Graves and Mary Renault, "but also dragged in Gore Vidal (why?)."

Whether or not Professor Moore realized it—one

would like to think he edits so many books that he forgets the authors' names—he was alluding to my *Saturday Review* piece. In the interest of truth, for what little it is worth today, I did not "drag in" Gore Vidal; I merely said that few novels about classical antiquity had any literary merit, the notable exceptions being *I, Claudius, Hadrian's Memoirs, The Last of the Wine,* and Vidal's *Julian.*

It is strange that the very mention of Vidal's name produced such a response from Professor Moore, who could not distinguish between a legitimate reference to a novel and a gratuitous allusion to a novelist. Yet in the academic world this kind of reaction is typical. Basically it comes down to asking, "Why Gore Vidal?" One can only answer this tiresome question by posing others: Why Chaucer or Shakespeare, when it seems everything that could have been said about them has been said? Why Herrick or Herbert, "minor poets" and therefore ideally suited to doctoral dissertations? Why . . . why anybody?

But specifically, why Gore Vidal?

I started reading Vidal when I was in college in the mid-fifties, about ten years after he began publishing. Most college students of that era who were eager to know what was happening in contemporary literature pursued their interests without a mentor. Except for an occasional and apologetically offered course in the Modern Novel (from *The Return of the Native* to *A Portrait of the Artist as a Young Man*) or Modern Poetry (from Hopkins to Eliot), one slaked his thirst for relevance in the public library, since the college library had more critical studies than works of fiction. The "serious" littérateurs on campus thumbed through the *Saturday Review of Literature,* while awaiting the arrival of the Sunday *New York Times,* which then meant only Section 2 and the *Book*

Review; yes, we were apolitical, as the Aquarians charged. Those of us who did not live in the New York area read the Sunday *Times* on Monday afternoon in the alcove of the reference section, where it lay on an oblong table, its bulk illuminated by diffused sunlight. For us the *Times* was the Holy Grail, and it was only fitting that it should be spotlighted.

It was a lonely existence. We talked among ourselves of Hemingway and Salinger, that mighty diarchy, wishing our teachers who excoriated modern literature would say something, even by way of an *obiter dictum,* about an author we were reading, just to assure us they knew he existed; and perhaps an admission of Salinger's existence would confirm our own. But there was always silence, except for one occasion when an elderly professor who had stumbled upon *From Here to Eternity* devoted an entire period to attacking it, becoming so tongue-tied he confused James Jones with James Joyce.

Yet the solitary life had certain compensations; in the absence of tutelage, one read at random, the only way to acquire any foundation in literature. Then contemporary fiction had no connection with the Academy; one read the masters in school, the moderns at home. It was an unstructured approach, somewhat bipolar and, in retrospect, preferable to getting college credit for something that was truly "independent study."

In 1955, my literary promiscuity was bringing me to T-U-V in the card catalogue. A friend suggested I read Sigrid Undset, but since she was not an American (we were patriotic then), I decided to forgo that pleasure for a while. I knew Gore Vidal's name from his television plays and also from John W. Aldridge's *After the Lost Generation,* the only critical book I could find on the moderns. Trained in the Classics (what else was there, we were told), I adhered to chronology and began with *Williwaw*, his first novel. At the time I thought—and my opinion has not changed—*The Naked and the Dead* was more impressive. Yet *Williwaw* was a tour de force for a nineteen-year-old, the average age of the college freshman. As one who was taught to believe, however erroneously, that a college education was the prerequisite for any career, I was amazed that Gore Vidal, whose formal schooling ended when he left Phillips Exeter Academy in 1943, could write such a fine novel without benefit of an "Introduction to Literature" course.

Since the mid-fifties, I have followed Vidal's career with all its vicissitudes. It is a career that uniquely affirms the right of the American man of letters to venture into any literary form he chooses, to cut across genres if necessary and court whatever muse is currently beckoning. Thus far, Gore Vidal has produced an impressive body of work: fiction, essays, television scripts, scenarios, Broadway plays. Obviously everything he has written is not equally memorable. All one can ask of a writer like Vidal is that he produce something of value in each field he enters. I believe he has.

It is becoming increasingly clear that the young American writer will pursue a similarly diversified career, reflecting in his work the spirit of egalitarianism that is now manifesting itself on the campus in the form of open admissions, free universities, work-study programs, and the "drop back" (as opposed to the "drop out") philosophy of education. Knowledge is growing less specialized, and the generalist is gradually being given the dignity that was once reserved solely for the scholar. Joyce Carol Oates has already begun to distribute her myriad energies throughout the literary spectrum, ignoring the critics who beg her to slow down or write in one genre. Today, one can no more tell a young author to perfect one medium and then dabble in others than one can tell a student to remain in college for four years or to major in English if he wants to write. It is clearly the time for options. The traditionalists will drone on, asking where the scholars will come from; yet they will come when they realize they are destined for scholarship, not creativity.

Why Gore Vidal? I trust *The Apostate Angel* will answer a question that in a more humane age would never be asked.

My approach to Vidal's career has been, for the most part, chronological, except for Chapter 8, "The Political Animal," which covers the period from 1960 (the year Vidal ran for Congress and prepared *The Best Man* for Broadway) to 1972 (*An Evening with Richard Nixon and . . .*). When I discuss *The City and the Pillar, Dark Green, Bright Red, The Judgment of Paris*, and *Messiah*, I am referring to the *revised* versions. I doubt that anyone will read the 1948 *City and the Pillar* today except as a comparative exercise; while the 1965 *City and the Pillar Revised* claimed to be a total rewrite, it was still the same novel with a different ending, a tighter style, and a less rabid attitude toward the American Mother. Someday a doctoral student will provide a scholarly analysis of Vidal's revisions, although I frankly do not believe the revised editions differ that radically from the originals.

The essays pose a different problem. In 1972, Vidal told an interviewer for the *Atlantic Monthly* his novels were "twice as good" as his essays. He also believes his essays, which comprise book and theatre reviews, literary criticism, and political journalism are the product of "many different occasions and moods." Because a writer's nonfiction often illuminates his fiction, I have decided not to treat the essays separately (which would be virtually impossible) but to integrate them with a discussion of the novels. Vidal prefers this method, and in writing about a living author, one should accede to a request that is not unreasonable.

Since Vidal has expressed himself openly in his essays and interviews, I have provided documentation for every statement of his that I quote. Between the fall of 1971 and the spring of 1972, I interviewed Vidal myself on several occasions. Statements of Vidal's which are not documented should be interpreted as comments made to me during that period.

Teaneck, New Jersey
July 18, 1973

1

A Portrait of the Artist as G. I. Joe

DURING A SEMINAR in Literary Theory, a visiting professor, so distinguished he was virtually unread, proposed what many students considered the critical dictum of the age: "One should no more begin a study of an author with his apprentice work than one should end a sentence with a preposition." Yet we have all done both, and often together. Usage now allows us to say, "I know the magazine you write for," and sheer perversity, dignified by the title of *Forschung*, sanctions our sleuthing around libraries and reading high school journals.

At first there is something wickedly exhilarating about examining a novelist's juvenilia, especially when the novelist is the author of *Myra Breckinridge*. Perhaps a phallic object in an early story is the forerunner of Myra's dildo. What a boon that would be for scholarship!

And so one dutifully obtains Volumes IX and X of the *Phillips Exeter Review* (1941–43), hoping for a scoop that will lead at least to a daytime talk show, if not to Johnny Carson. But there are no sexually ambiguous tales, no androgynous preppies, and worse, no embryonic dildos. There are only the poems and short stories of an adolescent who satirized, wondered, and despaired like the generations before him that called themselves lost.

He was not Gore Vidal then; that name would come later. He was merely Gene Vidal, who enrolled at Phillips Exeter Academy in the fall of 1940 and the following year published two poems in the *Review*. Gene Vidal was barely sixteen, a bit unsure of his metrics, and not totally convinced of mutability:

> The years have come, like night
> Have fled, yet still the tower stands,
> Bathed in the moon's cold light
> Glistening on the sands.
> —"Tower of Stone" (1941)

A teen-age agnostic damned from here to eternity, he bleated like all the lambs who ever went astray:

> Night, night black as the wills of men;
> We are lost to hope and God;
> For the chosen, we the chosen, there is no start, no end;
> Evil spirits that shall never yield nor bend
> Save for the soul of night, not the rod.
> For the night is black,
> No light but night,
> No God.
> —"To R. K. B.'s Lost Generation" (1941)

Gene Vidal was the poet who fell upon the thorns of life and bled, but Gore was the satirist who would inflict that fate on others. By the fall of 1942, the *Phillips Exeter Review* was publishing the stories of one Gore Vidal; Gene had disappeared, presumably into that "night black as the wills of men" that enveloped young poets, and Gore replaced him as Exeter's answer to Robert Benchley. No doubt believers in oedipal rivalry would argue that the only child of Eugene Luther Vidal and Nina Gore Vidal destroyed his paternal *imago* and rechristened himself with his mother's family name. And perhaps there are those who would equate Vidal's transformation with Myra's: Gene/Gore Vidal = Myron/Myra Breckinridge. Regardless, "Gore Vidal" had, as the Hollywood moguls used to say, class; "Gene Vidal" did not.

Gore Vidal of the patrician name published three stories in the *Phillips Exeter Review* that should confirm what already seems axiomatic of the adolescent writer in the twentieth century: he compensates for his lack of experience by plucking the fruit of the modern Tree of Knowledge—the Movies. In "Mostly about Geoffrey" (1942), Vidal adhered to the basic premise of Universal's horror films and had his Wolf Man revert to human form when he was killed. "The Bride Wore a Business Suit" (1943), a marquee-made title that would have delighted the late Irving Thalberg, depicted a shotgun wedding of an Exeter lad to a girl he defiled with nothing more than a kiss. And Myra would have endorsed "New Year's Eve" (1943) as readily as the Hollywood stars endorsed Lux Toilet Soap; it was a glossy vignette about a colonel's wife, an artifact at forty-seven, literally swept off her feet (" 'I'm a fool, a fool . . .' ") by a young lieutenant, to the strains of Cole Porter's "Night and Day."

Vidal was such a literary celebrity at Phillips Exeter that he attracted the attention of future novelist John

Knowles, who entered the Academy in the fall of 1941. Although they never met, Knowles used the junior poet-orator as the model for Brinker Hadley in *A Separate Peace* (1959), the end-of-innocence novel that vied with *The Catcher in the Rye* and *Lord of the Flies* as the campus best seller of the sixties. Brinker, the class politician, Betty Grable fan, and advocate of retributive justice, also composed poetry. But his monometrical contribution to the war effort, "The War/Is a Bore," was a far cry from Vidal's songs of melancholy. Should future biographers care to pursue the similarities between Brinker and Vidal, they might remember that prep school literati are always objects of satire; as characters in fiction, they tend to be as creepy as the ivy-spun buildings on their campus.

In June 1943, Vidal was graduated from Phillips Exeter Academy where, by his own admission, he spent three of the happiest years of his life; by the end of July, he had joined the Enlisted Reserve Corps of the United States Army:

I went from prep school to an Army training program. Efforts to make an engineer of me failed, and I was sent as a private to the Army Air Corps.[1]

Disgruntled at the prospect of putting colored pins in maps, he learned there was a shortage of maritime officers in the Army Transportation Corps. Accordingly, he memorized a book on navigation, passed the required exam, and at eighteen became Gore Vidal, W 2139622, Warrant Officer Junior Grade (Technician specialist— Maritime), assigned to the F. S. 35 in the Aleutians.

In December 1944, Vidal began *Williwaw* during a run

between Chernowski Bay and Dutch Harbor; he continued working on his novel at Anchorage, Los Angeles, and Fort Dix, completing it in New York nine months later. "With the finishing of this book, my life as a writer began."[2]

Written when he was nineteen and published when he was twenty, *Williwaw* (1946) still holds some appeal for the author. Sixteen years after its publication, Vidal could still look back on it with admiration. There were flaws, of course. The rivalry of two maritime officers over a Norwegian whore did not constitute the most original of plots; and the style, so laconic the author seemed to be speaking through zippered lips that muffled any embellishments, was not especially literary. It was a borrowed style, sometimes from Hemingway, sometimes from the movies, with sequences masquerading as chapters.

Williwaw is the kind of novel where ravens circle ominously overhead and where a discarded pillowcase becomes a symbol of unrequited love. And despite all of its clichés—the stereotyped passengers on the ship of fools, the fragmentary prophecies that are always fulfilled, the fade-out where the anti-hero goes to a new life against a blue sky and a glittering sun—"it still works," as Vidal confidently noted.

And it works because Vidal overcame the temptation to write an art novel and fictionalized instead what did or could happen in the Aleutians during the winter of 1944–45. A freighter is making a run between Andrefski Bay and Arunga; it will take three days, the ideal period for a *rite de passage.* The crew comprises Evans, the skipper, a Sea Wolf at twenty-five; Smitty, the Indian cook; John Martin, the first mate, glib, roguish, collegiate but not college-educated—in short, the young Vidal; Duval, the chief engineer, and Bervick, the second mate, locked in rivalry over a Dutch Harbor slut. One has seen them all before in an infinity of war movies, and no doubt one will see them again when the cinema reclaims its heritage of stereotypy from television.

The passengers are equally familiar: Major Barkison, who, it is intimated, is due for a promotion to lieutenant colonel (he gets it at the end); Father O'Mahoney, Barry Fitzgerald at sea, whose primary concern is whether anyone is a Catholic; and Lieutenant Hodges, prissy and pink-faced, who blushes at paintings of nudes. The time is winter, the season of the williwaw (the Indian name for a storm peculiar to the Aleutians) which is mentioned so frequently one expects it to form the climax of the novel, "not unlike" (to use Myra's favorite litotes) John Ford's *The Hurricane* (1937).

But the williwaw was not the climax, nor was it even described climactically. The description is almost imagistic. Most first novelists would have erupted into a narrative torrent when the storm swept down on the freighter; or they would have aimed at epic grandeur, taking their cue from the tempest in the *Aeneid*, where the firmament explodes with lightning and waves rise to the stars. Having just seen Boris Karloff in *Isle of the Dead* (1945), Vidal followed the aesthetics of film, shooting the sequence in black and white instead of narrating it in swirling prose. He cut from Martin thrown across the wheelhouse to Evans scrambling across the water-slick deck. He juxtaposed a shot of a dog whining in the fo'c's'le with one of the mast splintering in the wind. The camera pans and tilts, moving inexorably to the supreme close-up of the ship lodged between two rocks.

The williwaw was expected, and it occurred with the

inevitability of a dark prophecy, leaving a battered ship, a dented ventilator, but no deaths. But something else was also inevitable—the confrontation between Bervick and Duval. The fires of resentment had been consuming both of them since the trip began. They argued over whether the cutting edge of a knife should face the plate and whether seals were fish or mammals. But their squabbles only concealed the real source of contention— Olga, who gave herself freely to Bervick, whom she tolerated, and sold herself to Duval, whom she desired. After the storm, Bervick attempts to repair the ventilator. Duval's taunts and his impatient outburst (" 'Well, hurry up and get that thing nailed' ") become the last thrust of the knife. Bervick flings a hammer at his rival, knocking him overboard.

In this, the novel's real climax, Vidal goes beyond cinema, or at least the cinema of his youth. Bervick is not even charged with involuntary manslaughter because the men keep clannishly silent. The would-be tragedy collapsed as swiftly as the house of cards Lieutenant Hodges was building when the incident occurred. The novel reverses itself, almost as if Vidal remembered William Dean Howells' advice to "concentrate on the more smiling aspects of life, which are the more American." The ending is as American as a cinematic rainbow arching over the horizon while THE END centers itself on the screen. It is also an ending as American as that of Stephen Crane's *The Red Badge of Courage* (1895), which Vidal readily admits influenced him:

Over the river a golden ray of sun came through the hosts of leaden rain clouds.

—The Red Badge of Courage

The sky was blue and clear now and the sun shone on the white mountains. They walked back to the ship.

—*Williwaw*

At the end of Crane's novel, Henry Fleming has successfully completed his initiation into manhood, symbolized by a solitary ray of sun emerging through the leaden clouds. War was also the medium of Bervick's *rite de passage*, but it was a war fought on three fronts: Bervick was not only defending his country against the enemy but also his integrity against the double threat of Olga's fickleness and Duval's overpowering virility. Duval's death becomes Bervick's transfiguration, and the novel ends with the familiar tranquillity that follows the storm; or in Bervick's case, with a sunburst of manhood that illuminates the scales of justice while darkening them at the same time.

For all its cinematic touches, *Williwaw* "still works," particularly on the amoral level. Vidal had not yet met André Gide, but one senses *le maître* would have approved of Bervick's going off scot-free to a brighter tomorrow. He did not really perform Gide's "gratuitous act" nor did he commit homicide, but perhaps something of both. However, John W. Aldridge, one of the better evaluators of the post-World War II American novel, was somewhat disturbed by the resolution, arguing that the crew's loyalty to Bervick was "without a basis in moral action."[3]

Although art and morality have always been strange bedfellows, Vidal presumably did not set out to write an amoral novel; he was merely exploring the microcosm of war—the loneliness that results when physical proximity becomes a substitute for camaraderie, and the moral ambiguity that arises when ordinarily reprehensible actions become allowable, even necessary, to preserve human dignity. *Williwaw* was a sort of elegiac *Story of G. I. Joe*, somewhere between a hymn to the survivor and a threnody for the misbegotten. Long before the anti-hero became a synonym for nuclear man, Vidal understood his dilemma: the heroic need for excellence, even in so limited an area as maintaining a whore's fidelity, versus the barbaric urge to defend that carefully demarcated terrain against invaders. Bervick cannot be blamed for Duval's death; it was a petty war crime sanctioned by a military code that rewarded those who sacrificed their integrity in the call of duty. Bervick simply questioned a code which made the killing of the enemy honorable but which ignored the possibility that the enemy could be a fellow officer. He therefore wrote his own manual in the best tradition of military expediency.

Except for the dénouement, there is something atypical about *Williwaw*; it hardly seems the work of Gore Vidal, The Count of the Late-Night Talk Shows, or Lily Tomlin's effete "Mr. Veed'l" of *Laugh-In*. Detached as the writing is, it does not conceal the author's compassion for his characters, most of whom were his intellectual inferiors. Only John Martin, the most erudite member of the crew, remains unsympathetic because he is so magnificently irrelevant. When he is not reading perfumed letters or lurid magazines, he is playing the cool lover, the inadequate seaman, or a smart-assed Greek chorus. Was Martin Vidal's persona, as we say in Academe? If so, it is commendable that at nineteen Gore Vidal knew a persona's function was to keep the author from becoming a bore.

John Martin was twenty-four during his three-day

initiation into the rites of winter. Should the reader wonder what happened to him (he disappeared from the plot as swiftly as the williwaw), he was discharged, moved to New York, and became Robert Holton of *In a Yellow Wood* (1947)—twenty-six, a gifted amateur destined or doomed to success on Wall Street because of his ability to be amorphous and his inability to love.

Williwaw was a young soldier's novel; *In a Yellow Wood* was a young writer's, complete with an epigraph from Robert Frost's "The Road Not Taken": "Two roads diverged in a yellow wood,/And sorry I could not travel both/And be one traveler . . ." Naturally yellow will be the dominant color in a novel that spans the proverbial one-day of Greek drama. The Indian summer sun "glowed yellowly"; secretaries have yellow hair; an aging waitress yearns for a yellow satin dress; an artificial yellow suffuses Holton's hotel room; and significantly, he is employed by the firm of Heywood & Golden, "the yellow wood" into which he wanders. It is the plutocrat's color emblazoned on a novel whose hero is so obsessed with making money that he unabashedly admits it to everyone, including his employer.

In a Yellow Wood is a peculiarly American novel, right down to the name of Robert Holton. His is the dream name with which all Americans should be christened, easily pronounced and neatly syllabified. In fact, most of Vidal's characters—John Martin, Jim Willard, Peter Nelson, Philip Warren, and of course, Myra Breckinridge—belong to that raceless, creedless, and colorless aristocracy where names are honorifics with no trace of an immigrant background or an ethnic association.

Robert Holton is a peculiarly American type: the war hero returning to the lethargy of peace, the ex-Harvard playboy forced to choose between love and money, the young executive sorting out his masks for the day—a face for the menials, one for the colleagues, and still another for the bosses. Yet all of Holton's masks merge into one, with slits wide enough to accommodate vacant eyes and a cavity hollow enough for a gaping mouth. He makes small talk with the elevator operator, with lonely waitresses and secretaries, even with the celebrities he meets at a cocktail party. The rhythms are always the same— jerkily precise, prosaically unequivocal: " 'See you then.' " " 'Ready to go?' " " 'That's fine.' " " 'It's not much fun, living alone.' " " 'I'd like to make more money.' " His is a repertoire too innocuous to be cynical, too telegraphic to be ambivalent.

Holton is all shadow and no substance, or to be more charitable, a human photon. He rises in a West Side hotel room and prepares for a typical day on Wall Street, first checking his comb for falling hair and worrying briefly about the effect a sedentary job will have on his physique. The morning and afternoon pass uneventfully, except for a visit from an army buddy, Jim Trebling. Their meeting is awkward; Trebling came to renew an old acquaintance and found instead a reserved Holton who was so uptight he reminded his friend that smoking was prohibited in the office.

" 'You remember the time we were in Florence?' " Jim asks.[4] Such a question in a scenario is the cue for a flashback, and so it is in the novel, where the brokerage house dissolves to wartime Florence, where Holton first met Carla, his dark lady. An Italian beauty is rarely dredged up from the Waters of Oblivion and then submerged. One will meet her again.

At five-thirty the working day ended, or so it did in

1947, and Holton returned to Central Park West. "In the evenings the Park was the most peaceful place in the city," or so it was in 1947, when the subway fare was also a nickel. Nothing dates faster than Manhattan. Holton goes off to Helena Stevanson's cocktail party, where the two roads of Frost's poem appear and suddenly bifurcate.

Holton's Boston background makes Mrs. Stevanson's world accessible to him. It also makes the *roman à clef* accessible to Vidal. *In a Yellow Wood* is one of those vaguely autobiographical novels where the author translates the drudgery of an editorship he held briefly at E. P. Dutton and Company in 1946 into the diurnal boredom of a brokerage house. However, there are differences between Vidal and his ill-fitting persona; the author detested office jobs and left publishing after *Williwaw* became a success, while his character thrived on routine and encamped permanently in the yellow wood of Wall Street.

Vidal describes Mrs. Stevanson's party in much the same way, first suggesting a few similarities between a character and his historical counterpart (soundalike names, idiosyncrasies) and then confounding the reader with pieces from an entirely different puzzle. George *Robert* (italics Vidal's) Lewis, the editor of a pretentious journal called *Regarde*, is at the party; his middle name was Gallicized as was that of Charles *Henri* (italics mine) Ford, dilettante, belletrist, moviemaker, and editor of the avant-garde but historically significant *View*.

Then there is Carla Blankton, the Florentine *donna* Holton met during the war, now married to a painter and wealthy enough to afford what our hero can not. Vidal admits in private the model for Carla was Anaïs

Nin, the butterfly of the literary underground, who tried to teach the young author how to "flow." But Nin was not a Florentine, and more important, Carla was not a diarist.

While it may be interesting to know the historical equivalents of the literati, the establishment of their identities does little more than make the novel a mildly intriguing *roman à clef.* Either the individuals in real life were as unsubstantial as their fictional counterparts or Vidal could not find their third dimension. Whatever the case, *In a Yellow Wood* is a young man's novel, where the obvious becomes the subtle by the italicization of a middle name and where a visit to a transvestite night club becomes a descent to the underworld.

Telling the reading public that homosexuality is a recurrent theme in Vidal's fiction is almost like explaining to musicologists that the leitmotif is Richard Wagner's trademark. Three of the seven short stories in *A Thirsty Evil* (1956) concern homosexuality. In "Three Stratagems" (1950), an epileptic male prostitute cruises Key West, not so much to hustle rich old men as to satisfy their need for degradation. The milieu has its own language, where syntax is cryptogram and ellipsis. An aging buyer introduces himself to a pickup by informing him that he was married (but now is a widower), that the hotel where he is staying is one of the best, and that the proprietor is extremely tolerant. In "The Zenner Trophy" (1950), which is also written so cautiously that only the aura of homosexuality is present but never the word or the act, two star athletes are expelled from prep school for practicing something the faculty is too shocked to define. "Pages from an Abandoned Journal" (1956), written especially for the collection, describes a young historian torn between heterosexuality and homosexuality; he chooses the latter, abandons his studies at Columbia, and takes a job selling antique furniture, presumably to gain access to the clientele he desires.

The homoerotics in *The City and the Pillar*, the steambath rendezvous in *The Judgment of Paris*, the boys on the bathroom floor in *Washington, D.C.*, and a visit to Proust's favorite male brothel in *Two Sisters* are sufficient reason, for the time being, to conclude that Vidal has more than a casual interest in the subject.

The night club where Lewis takes Carla and Holton affords Vidal his first opportunity to describe the gay demimonde as seen through the hero's dazed eyes. Carla knows immediately what kind of club it is and has the sudden desire to protect her lover's innocence. She is familiar with the milieu because of her husband, whose tendencies are disclosed elliptically in that moment of truth where each syllable of the revelation is inflected with the same gravity: " 'He was . . . was . . . like these people here.' " Shocking by 1947 standards, just kinky today.

Lewis is a habitué, quite impressed by a dancer with the bizarre name of Hermes de Bianca, whose solo combines Martha Graham's psychic contortions with Gypsy Rose Lee's bumps and grinds. Religion and art seem to be the perennial topics of discussion among homosexuals, and when Hermes joins their table, he promptly confesses his desire to become a Catholic, or as he phrases it in the idiom of the catechumens, "to go to Rome."

After his initiation, Holton brings Carla to his hotel room, where they engage in that beatific coition that occurs when the rhythms of sex have been judiciously separated from the act:

He entered her and to the rhythm of their fast-beating hearts, with a rush of sound like wind in his ears, he discovered the single world. Lights whirled inside his head, behind his eyes; they came in series—circles of sharp lights. (pp. 186–87)

The episode is one of the most sensuous Vidal has written. He has caught the rhythms of love, the exulting rise and the dying fall, the exchange of roles where lover and beloved merge, the "colored lights" (as Stanley Kowalski called them) whirling concentrically toward infinity, the agony and the ecstasy and the quiescence. The metaphors may be a bit mixed; Holton, "a giant in a world of giant sensations," becomes "shipwrecked" between Carla's thighs, like Captain Cat in Dylan Thomas' *Under Milk Wood* (1954). But the overall effect was one of understated eroticism, something the author would not achieve again.

"The time has come to speak about love," Carson McCullers wrote in *The Ballad of the Sad Café* (1943). And after making *grand amore*, the participants now talk about it. Carla advocates freedom through love and offers herself as the source of that freedom. Naturally her offer is rejected.

Most scenarios of the 1940's, however grim their subjects were, held out the prospect of happiness as if the alternative were too catastrophic to consider. In the best MGM tradition Holton wins a promotion, which should more than adequately compensate for a love that made too many demands and a friendship that demanded nothing.

In a Yellow Wood was dedicated to Anaïs Nin, whose philosophy of love, as a sort of fluid algebra where man and woman combine like x and y to form the square root of wonderful, sufficiently impressed Vidal to incorporate it into some of Carla's reflective dialogue. By the end of the 1960's, if not sooner, Vidal had grown weary of her girlish romanticism. Instead of dismissing it like an antique that time had declared fraudulent, he parodied it in *Two Sisters* (1970) in the character of the Nin-like memoirist, Marietta Donegal, who also believed "we must flow deeply from the core of our inner being."

In 1971, Anaïs Nin published the fourth volume of her *Diary*, that strangely self-generating work where some of the most creative people of the century floated in the waters of a womb that was not capacious enough to contain them. The authors who gravitated to Nin, her "children," as she called them, were more like orphans adopted by a mother who would not accept their maturity even on those rare occasions when it manifested itself. Yet the diaries, despite their rhetorical questions ("Did I imagine this Gore?") and pubescent sensibility, have a fascination most memoirs lack. The outsider can never prove their veracity, but he can enter the diarist's soul—a soul so feminine it grows more uterine with each installment.

Vidal plays a major role in Volume IV, which covers the period from 1944 to 1947. He met Nin for the first time in the fall of 1945 at Kimon Friar's lecture at the Y.M.H.A.:

The lieutenant leaned over and introduced himself: "I am Warrant Officer Gore Vidal. I am a descendant of Troubadour Vidal."[5]

For a time Vidal played Attis to Nin's Cybele. He got Dutton to publish her novel *Ladders to Fire* (1946), which was dedicated to him, while Nin in turn gave Vidal a maternalism he had never known. But the Cybele of American Letters and her *enfant terrible* were as ill-matched as Lesbia and Catullus. *Odi et amo* sums up both couples. Vidal could no more accept Nin's non-intellectualism ("I never generalize, intellectualize") than she could accept the loveless sex in the novels that followed *In a Yellow Wood.* For a time Vidal tried to "flow," but the current was too strong. He enjoyed wearing his persona and resisted Nin's attempts to unmask him so he could join the playpen with her "other children."

In 1970 the Madonna cabled her erstwhile child in Rome for permission to print her memories of their relationship in Volume IV. When they met in Paris, Nin at sixty-seven was no less maternal; she chided Vidal on her portrait in *Two Sisters,* adding by way of further admonishment: "I didn't read it, of course—I don't read that sort of book—but I was told it was a hideous caricature."[6] Vidal placated the Mother Goddess by explaining that Marietta was not Anaïs, although their interest in flowing was somewhat similar. The Mother Goddess was apparently satisfied: "Anyway you said—I was told —that I wrote well."

In a Yellow Wood, intended as an examination of the masks people wear, became a dissection of the games people play. Vidal never revised the novel as he did several of the others. "It was never the book I wanted to write. *She* entered it, and then it was too late."

2

Huck Honey
on the Potomac

IN DECEMBER 1946, Anaïs Nin read the manuscript of Vidal's third novel, *The City and the Pillar* (1948). Appalled by its cynicism, she felt obliged to record her thoughts for posterity:

He is only twenty years old. He writes a book on a one-dimensional world, sex in a void. A book which will hurt his possibilities in the political world. A prosaic and literal book. The editor at Dutton said: "I hate it." (*The Diary*, p. 175)

Actually, Vidal had turned twenty-one, but no matter. At the time he regarded it as his greatest novel and begged Nin to concur. She would not, for Childe Gore had once again defaced the wallpaper in the nursery.

The novel is no longer one of the author's favorites, yet he felt strongly enough about it to revise it in 1965, adding an "Afterword" and changing the ending from strangulation to sodomy—an alteration which caused a radio reviewer to remark that Vidal knew more about homosexuality in 1965 than he did in 1948.

In 1943 Vidal knew enough about it to attempt a novel about a homosexual writer. Among the memorabilia he deposited with The State Historical Society of Wisconsin at Madison is a 175-page typescript simply entitled *A Novel;* on the title page, the author has written the following: "nearly finished—begun at Exeter '43—continued at V.M.I. [Virginia Military Institute][1] fall of '43 —*abandoned.*"

In *A Novel*, the life of an American man of letters, James R. Morison, is narrated in flashback by three men who have come to attend his funeral: Caleb, his college roommate; Guy Brooke, his first lover; and Fernald, his publisher. Each reconstructs the dead man's past with little feeling, for he was not the sort to inspire affection in anyone, including his wife of seven months. Each had accepted Morison's homosexuality with varying degrees of tolerance, but no one was quite prepared for his will, which left everything to a tennis player.

Except for a few poetic passages in *The City and the Pillar*, Vidal has never approached homosexuality with either Genêt's lyrical rapture or Gide's silken diabolism. It is calculated barter where the language of exchange does not even require a translator's ear for idiom. Only to adolescents, thrown into each other's arms from fear of estrangement, is Vidal sympathetic; it is assumed that consenting adults are beyond pathos.

To the eighteen-year-old Vidal, love between males was neither the dark underside of human passion nor the dappled glory of youth. It was merely one of nature's givens and therefore completely amoral, as Morison tried to explain to Caleb: "Always remember, Caleb, that people can't help being what they were created. You were born liking women; I was not. I like you the way you are. I don't think I would have had you different." (p. 51)

After Morison moved in with Guy Brooke, the two lovers did exactly what the Platonic youths did in E. M. Forster's *Maurice*—they *talked*, and not even in the same bed. *A Novel* is almost all talk, much of it impeccably rendered. The characters speak to each other, not to converse but to shape their ideas into dialogue. When Vidal is describing a *fin de siècle* homosexual milieu, he treats it the way Henry James would treat a drizzle or a snowfall—as one of nature's more ordinary manifestations one vaguely recognizes but never allows to overwhelm the individual consciousness. In fact, *A Novel* is often reminiscent of James' *The Pupil* or *The Bostonians*, where sexual ambiguity is always present, hidden behind the portières but banished from the drawing room and unthinkable in the boudoir.

The final segment of *A Novel* is an excerpt from Morison's autobiography that stands as a noble corrective to the Somerset Maugham image he conveyed to his friends. The prose is prismatic and exact, qualities that have always been associated with Vidal. It is ultimately poignant, for Vidal has revealed more of himself in this portion than he might care to admit. The fictional autobiography was a self-fulfilling prophecy: what Morison disclosed about himself has come to pass in Vidal's own life—a fondness for Italy as a colorful refuge from Anglo-Saxon drabness, a basic dislike of the theatre although he achieved some success in it, an apathy toward people because they were never what he wanted them to be, a boredom that comes when a sure-fire literary formula has been perfected, and particularly an insistence on some artistic standards in a world gone mad with realism:

It has become the custom of writers today (1939) to reproduce with painful thoroughness the conversation of uneducated people; this is called realism. These writers are capable of going on for pages with profanity and boring repetition. It is quite true that people don't often finish their sentences and are apt to repeat themself [*sic*], and those people are usually quite boring. A writer who tries to do a word-by-word reproduction of such a conversation commits the most inexcusable sin in literature: he becomes an uninformative bore. (p. 156)

Vidal's views on sloppy prose have not changed since he was eighteen. The writers he then called "boring" are now "demotic."

Morison was a born man of letters, striving for a perfection in his work that would compensate for the disorder of life. He was a gifted teller of tales, a writer of sophisticated comedy, and an occasional novelist of substance. When he published a work of depth, it was damned for its sexual frankness; one thinks immediately of *The City and the Pillar*, which *The New York Times* refused to advertise. Morison was as proud of publishing three books in three years as Vidal was of producing six in five years (two of which came out within ten months of each other in 1950). Although Morison vacillated between being the critics' darling and their whipping boy, he did not need their reviews to remind him of his accomplishments and his limitations:

I have written a great deal in the last half-century. I have been rightly called prolific, but I do not consider that term derogatory either. Writing is my profession and I practice it as such, and I am seldom not working. I have written some very bad books, I am at least aware they are bad; I flatter myself perhaps that I have written a few good novels and plays. (p. 163)

A Novel was not only an amazing achievement for an eighteen-year-old; it was also a blueprint for the author's later life.

It is interesting to speculate how Vidal's career would have fared if he had reworked the Morison story and published it as his first novel. *The City and the Pillar* might have created less of a furor, and the critics could have lamented the degeneration of the author's style from Jamesian to Zolaesque instead of the degeneration of the author.

Now it is difficult to think of *The City and the Pillar* in terms of degeneration of any sort. Since the late forties, the American public has grown less parochial in its outlook on homosexuality. As boxer shorts no longer suggest virility, neither does membership in the Y.M.C.A. Today, in fact, it could denote the opposite. Consequently, *The City and the Pillar* with its once-subtle distinctions between shrill transvestites and manly lovers, sentimental queens and introspective dreamers, is no longer the Baedeker for anyone journeying through the circles of the gay inferno. Vidal simply charted the terrain which others have apportioned. Furthermore, his thesis in the "Afterword" that "all human beings are bisexual" is not so unnerving as it would have been in 1948. The parties in *The City and the Pillar*, where the inebriates pitch their voices toward a florid coloratura, are not much different from similar gatherings in university clubs or men's faculty lounges, where the talk never rises above a soporific bass. There is the same craning of necks, the close scrutiny of the outsider, the clucking disapproval of the iconoclast, and the fear of reprisal if one is the first to leave.

If *The City and the Pillar* were merely the father of contemporary homosexual fiction, one should only accord it the homage patriarchs usually receive—a quick nod or a hasty genuflection. But within the Vidal canon it occupies a more significant position: *The City and the Pillar* reworks material from *Williwaw* and *In a Yellow Wood* into the myth of natural man as the original homoerotic. In homosexuality, Vidal discovered a crucible that could melt down his first two novels to their components—sexual rivalry and the lost boyhood dream. In *Williwaw*, Vidal isolated Bervick's fastidiousness and Duval's bitchery in a military environment where men assumed characteristics traditionally attributed to women. *In a Yellow Wood* examined the dissolution of a friendship in terms of divergent careers. A homosexual sensibility was completely absent from both novels; yet their themes—a rivalry between males that reduces the contestants to epicene tormenters, a friendship that ends when paths no longer converge—could easily form the basis of a homosexual novel if they were united as cause and effect.

But if, as Leslie Fiedler argued in *Love and Death in the American Novel* (1960), there is constant ritual warfare between the female as the dark intruder and the male as the fair defender of a sacred boyhood, then there is an even closer connection between a brawl over a bedmate and the termination of a friendship. In *The City and the Pillar*, Vidal restored these motifs to their original form, where they were part of a homoerotic paradise myth—an all-male Eden that ripens with purity and rots with experience.

In his depiction of this paradise before and after the

fall, Vidal uses—and explodes—Mark Twain's symbols of the Mississippi boyhood: the cabin, the enchanted woods, the brown river, the barefoot boys defying mortality, and civilization as the meddling female. It is almost as if Vidal set out to write an anti-*Huckleberry Finn* merely to prove what Judge Brack said at the end of *Hedda Gabler:* "People don't do things like that!"

The godlike Mississippi is a dominant symbol in *The Adventures of Huckleberry Finn.* Significantly, *The City and the Pillar* begins and ends with the image of a river. The novel is a flashback framed by prologue and epilogue. In a New York bar, Jim Willard recalls a period from 1937 to 1943 as his fingers idly trace islands and rivers in the water that spilled from his drink. At first the crude cartography seems like drunken doodling, but out of the geography of reminiscence a watery Eden appears on a charred tabletop—a savage parody of the idyllic retreat where he first made love to Bob Ford.

By some planetary determinism, both *The City and the Pillar* and Leslie Fiedler's "Come Back to the Raft Ag'in, Huck Honey!" appeared in the same year—the novel in January 1948 (although it was written in 1946) and the essay on boyish homoeroticism in *Huck Finn, The Last of the Mohicans,* et al. in the June *Partisan Review.* In the essay, Fiedler alluded to "a recent book" of Vidal's where "an incipient homosexual, not yet aware of the implications of his feelings, indulges in the apt reverie of running off to sea with his dearest friend" (p. 669).

Melville, Cooper, and Twain projected the popular concept of male friendship in its purest form; but it was a dream that could only exist in a Neverland that was pastoral enough to unsex the youths who romped through it. Admit a woman to the sylvan paradise and the cool form of boyhood begins to glower; remove the Arcadian illusion and the form becomes flesh.

In *The City and the Pillar*, Bob invites Jim to spend a weekend in a cabin near the Potomac immediately after he announces he is taking a girl to a dance:

> "I'm taking old Sally Mergendahl to the dance tonight." He winked. "And tonight I mean to do myself some good."
> "Why not? Everybody else has." Jim disliked Sally, a dark aggressive girl who had been after Bob all year. But then it was none of his business what Bob did.
> As they walked through the blue twilight . . . Bob suddenly asked, "What're you doing this weekend?"
> "Nothing. Why?"
> "Why don't we spend it down at the cabin?"
> "Well, sure. Why not?"²

Jim's quick acceptance of the invitation is an attempt to displace the "dark aggressive" Sally, who would bring with her the matriarchal demands of marriage, monogamy, and worse, civilization. It is an unnecessary attempt, for Jim becomes the aggressive lover before Sally has a chance to play her role. Jim and Bob are the Good Bad Boys demythologized who cannot endure the limits of the classic American friendship. And the Virginia woods are no longer the sexless landscape of pastoral, but a literal bower of bliss. Vidal has subjected a fictional friendship to the acid test of reality, where it is impossible to live by the books. The dream yields to an incarnation too sacred for the real order, too profane for the archetypal. Even the author is powerless to give their new life anything more than poetic sanction. When Jim and Bob cease being model friends, Vidal uses one of the oldest devices in poetry to combine the joy of their momentary union with the sadness of its aftermath—the pathetic fallacy, where nature augments passion with a warm wind and then shares in the silence of lost innocence with a sudden calm:

So they met. Eyes tight shut against an irrelevant world. A wind warm and sudden shook all the trees, scattered the fire's ashes, threw shadows to the ground.
But then the wind stopped. The fire went to coals. The trees were silent. No comets marked the dark lovely sky, and the moment was gone. In the fast beat of a double heart, it died. (p. 41)

Since Jim and Bob have broken literary precedent by using the Arcadian playground for a lovers' tryst and exchanging the barrier of the handshake for the proximity of the body, they seek consolation in another American myth—the sea, with its mysterious power of restoring lost manhood. Bob ships off, and Jim follows a year later, embarking on a quest for his brother-lover that takes him from Virginia to the West Coast and finally back to the East for the moment of reckoning. But time has transformed the adolescent experiment into the grand passion. Since Jim can no longer be the dream lover, he assumes the role of the quester pursued by tempters who challenge the integrity of his vision.

In Seattle, he rejects a woman and rushes from her room, still convinced the fraternal paradise grows to seed when the female enters it. In Los Angeles, he becomes the lover of a middle-aged movie idol; their relationship is unsatisfying because Jim measures it against the ideal. Soon he is initiated into the milieu where he learns to differentiate between the straight and the gay; but the demimonde repels him because he has reworked the episode in the woods into a Theocritean pastoral that is too fragile for explication. Comparing the Hollywood queens with the Platonic form they have perverted, he wonders "how what had been so natural and complete for him could be so perfectly corrupted by these strange womanish creatures."

The search for the ideal leads him from Ronald Shaw the star to Paul Sullivan the novelist. Sullivan, the paradigm of the Catholic homosexual, is so guilt-ridden that his inability to experience fulfillment in love is a self-administered penance. While Sullivan's passion is as loveless as his novels, Jim finds something in it that at least approximates the goal—a reticence that is manly in its contempt for self-pity.

His liaison with Sullivan is short-lived. A woman appears, the "dark" Maria Verlaine, who desires Jim but, like Ronald Shaw, theorizes too much about love. He rejects her because she is the Death Goddess—Thanatos rather than Eros. An army stint during World War II exposes the quester to a different type of homosexual and further frustrates his search for the vanished dream. In his use of pseudo-masculine clichés (" 'We bachelors should stick together' "; " 'A guy can't be too careful' "), Vidal is merciless in his reproduction of a language that is self-decoding. A corporal's displeasure at a town full of queers becomes an invitation which Jim translates into the idiom he learned in Hollywood. But the corporal is a desultory bedmate because he is, as the platitude goes, promised to another—Sergeant Kervinski.

When the reconciliation finally occurs, Jim discovers that Bob's marriage to Sally Mergendahl precludes the possibility of reliving the weekend in the cabin. Rather than have the dream revert to a reverie one conjures up in time of loneliness, Jim transforms it into a nightmare by raping the friend who broke the boyhood taboo through marriage and fatherhood. In the 1948 version he strangled Bob and went out into the morning air as amorally fancy-free as Bervick in *Williwaw*. In the 1965 revision, the ending is a variation on André Gide's *l'acte gratuit*, where the hero commits an apparently meaningless act to achieve a dubious selfhood. This time there is no pathetic fallacy, no interweaving of man and nature, but simply the wish to punish an ex-lover who reduced the moment in the woods to the antics of "a couple of little queers."

Strangulation or rape—which is the more truthful? Either ending is merely the metaphorical reduction of love to a death gasp, the closing of the circle that began with breathing in unison and ended with the final exhalation of the one and the satisfied sigh of the other. The new ending is shocking only if taken literally. In both cases, love has moved from the frontier, the margin between (but unfortunately not beyond) good and evil, into an area where it can no longer be neutral. In exploding the American novel of friendship, Vidal has shattered the myth of chastity on which it was based. "The change of myth involves a profound change of meaning," as Leslie Fiedler cautioned.

The sea remains when the dream dies. Caught in the cycle of the eternal recurrence, Jim ships out to sea again, but the river that will carry him to it is not the archetypal "strong brown god" that T. S. Eliot called the Mississippi; it is a Lethe, "dark and cold," that awaits the disillusioned dreamer.

Those who cherish the notion of interlocking novels will be delighted by the names of the main characters in

The City and the Pillar—Jim and Bob, perhaps the alter egos of Jim and Bob of *In a Yellow Wood.* The novel was written in memory of J. T., enigmatic initials when one considers some of the other dedicatees: Anaïs Nin, Tennessee Williams, Christopher Isherwood, Lucien Price. From 1936 to 1939, Vidal attended St. Alban's in Washington, D.C., where one of his classmates was the school athlete, Jim Trimble, who was later killed at Iwo Jima and, like a *genius loci*, gave his name to a recreational center in Guam.

The young man who learns his boyhood friend has been killed in action is a familiar figure in Vidal's fiction. Bill Giraud of *The Season of Comfort* and Peter Sanford of *Washington, D.C.*, make the tragic discovery; Philip Warren in *The Judgment of Paris* can never forget the athlete, "a strong passionate boy," who died the year World War II ended. In "Pages from an Abandoned Journal," the penultimate story in *A Thirsty Evil*, the narrator tells a homosexual he meets in Paris "all about Jimmy . . . how it had started at twelve and gone on, without plan or thought or even acknowledgement until, at seventeen, I went to the Army and he to the Marines and a quick death."[3] Finally there is that haunting passage early in *Two Sisters*, one of the most eloquent Vidal has ever written, where he drops the cynic's mask and speaks directly to those who in adolescence endured the double agony of idolatry and infatuation, and in middle age developed into late-show weepers, confusing any soldier gone to the wars with the tender comrade himself:

Death, summer, youth—this triad contrives to haunt me every day of my life for it was in summer that my generation left school for war, and several dozen that one knew (but strictly speaking did not love, except perhaps for one) were killed, and so never lived to know what I have known—the Beatles, black power, the Administration of Richard Nixon—all this has taken place in a trivial aftertime and has nothing to do with anything that really mattered, with summer and someone hardly remembered, a youth . . . so abruptly translated from vivid, well-loved (if briefly) flesh to a few scraps of bone and cartilage scattered among the volcanic rocks of Iwo Jima . . . and one still mourns the past . . . watching the Late Show on television as our summer's war is again refought and one sees sometimes what looks to be a familiar face in the battle scenes—is it Jimmy?[4]

Yet any amount of biographical data cannot alter the fact that today *The City and the Pillar* is important as a mythic novel, not a homosexual one. The Hollywood that Jim Willard passed through was just a soundstage Babylon, and the patter of its denizens that once seemed so sophisticated is now as empty as the closets where they rehearsed for years. Ever since homosexuality became a regular topic of conversation on the talk shows, people have learned to distrust masculine bravado and to separate the lovers living quietly in the brownstones from the midnight cowboys in the Times Square corral. Mart Crowley's *The Boys in the Band* (1968) made the straightest of audiences see how a homosexual who was a practicing Catholic could need verbal flagellation from a Jew. A film like John Schlesinger's *Sunday Bloody Sunday* (1971), where a man and a woman share the same male lover, even received the endorsement of the National Catholic Office for Motion Pictures (formerly the Legion of Decency).

It is not entirely fair to say the changing times have given the book an antique veneer. *The City and the Pillar* was quaint in its day, although from some of the reviews that called it everything from "a male counterpart to *The Well of Loneliness*" to a "book on perverse practices," one would never know it was essentially an inversion of the American wilderness novel.

Far from proving that "all human beings are bisexual" (Jim Willard clearly was not), *The City and the Pillar* did prove that anyone who could crack the surface of *Huck Finn* and *The Last of the Mohicans* would eventually discover original sin. Vidal concluded it came into being when a pair of rebellious lads secularized the sacred rites of boyhood by enacting the forbidden parts of the rubrics. Read in the light of *Love and Death in the American Novel*, *The City and the Pillar* contains many of the recurrent themes Fiedler detected in Melville, Cooper, and Twain—the boyhood idyll, the intrusive woman, the miraculous sea, Cooper's redskin brother-surrogate for the white male in the guise of the red-haired Bob Ford, the lost frontier friendship. *The City and the Pillar* is the American wilderness novel demythologized; or rather it exposes the awesome truth the myth concealed.

3

Sons and Mothers

BY THE END of the 1940's, Gore Vidal had reached his own
bifurcating road. In one direction lay the privacy a novelist achieves only through depersonalization; in the
other, the familiarity he acquires from a signature that
never changes. The critics knew a familiar hand when
they saw it. In that *je ne sais quoi* way of theirs, they
sensed the first three novels were based on personal experience that had not been totally amalgamated into the
fictive; and John W. Aldridge really dented the persona
when he noted that in each novel "the characters . . .
were at about the same stage of development that Vidal
was when he conceived them."[1]

Every writer of fiction faces the dilemma of self-abne-
gation versus narcissism. Vidal solved it by painting others in broad strokes and by sketching himself in charcoal.

It was never the ideal solution, and even Anaïs Nin realized Vidal was using ordinary masks to conceal his extraordinary self. Although it was generally known that Gore Vidal was the Masked Marvel of Modern Letters, he had no intention of removing his visor, however translucent it was becoming.

Accordingly, he became a detached writer, the spokesman of "absolute spiritual nothingness," a parodist of the divine watchmaker presenting friendship and love as delicate mechanisms whose parts never functioned. Rivalry jarred the equilibrium, and self-interest shattered it. Vidal's despair that love could never be anything more than the ego's distorting mirror misled critics like Aldridge into imputing to the author "the aridity of soul" he implanted in his characters. And if it is true, as Aldridge also claims, that "Vidal has not yet created a single convincing female character," the reason may be that in his childhood he never encountered an especially convincing female.

Vidal wrote his fourth novel, *The Season of Comfort* (1949), as autobiographical a piece of fiction as one could find, as a partial explanation for the so-called spiritual desiccation of his work. It was almost as if he were asking the reviewers to ignore the New Critics, with their disdain of biography, and take a candid look at the family of the writer who "has not yet created a single convincing female character."

Like his fictional counterpart Bill Giraud, Gore Vidal was born into a political family. His father, Gene Vidal, to whom *The Season of Comfort* is dedicated, went through the *cursus honorum*, from South Dakota football hero to West Point instructor to cofounder of the airlines that are now Northeastern and TWA. During Franklin D.

Roosevelt's first term as president, he served as Director of Aeronautics in the Department of Commerce. In 1921, Gene Vidal married socialite Nina Gore, the daughter of the famous Senator Thomas Pryor Gore of Oklahoma. Four years later, on October 3, 1925, their son was born —Eugene Luther Gore Vidal, who at seventeen preferred to identify himself simply as Gore Vidal.

Shortly after their son's birth, the Vidals moved to Washington, D.C., to live with Senator Gore in his Rock Creek Park home. Because Senator Gore had been totally blind since the age of eleven, the young Vidal, beginning at the age of six, would read him the *Congressional Record*, constitutional law, Victorian poetry, even Eleanor Roosevelt's column, "My Day." At seven, he was leading his grandfather onto the floor of the Senate. He guided the Senator through museums, passing his fingers over the faces of the statues and reading off their titles and the sculptors' names. In turn, Senator Gore encouraged his grandson to roam freely through the attic library and call its northeast corner, with its vast collection of fairy tales, his own. In the "Author's Note" to *A Search for the King* (1950), Vidal has commented on his literary boyhood at Rock Creek Park:

From the time I was five and could read until I was ten or eleven and moved away, I read everything I could and ruined my eyes and cluttered my memory.

Vidal's impressions of the Rock Creek Park days were so indelible they became part of a scrapbook past of curled photographs and yellowed clippings that he could consult for reasons both literary and nostalgic. In "A Moment of Green Laurel" (1949), the third short story in

A Thirsty Evil, and written the year of Senator Gore's death, the narrator returns to Washington, D.C., for a presidential inauguration. Although he spent his youth there, the city is now as alien as the vulgarians he meets at an inaugural party and the mother from whom he is estranged. Familiar boyhood landmarks tap the springs of memory, and he wanders over to the old house in Rock Creek Park, where he comes upon a boy carrying a bouquet of laurel. Experience encounters innocence, or rather the man encounters the boy he once was. The twelve-year-old youth also had a grandfather whose attic library was his private cleft in the rock of the world. Like the narrator, the boy gravitated to history books and the *Arabian Nights*. And both picked laurel to make chaplets similar to those the Roman heroes wore in their favorite illustrated edition of Livy.

The years with Senator Gore fled so swiftly one could understand why Vidal wanted to relive them, if for no other reason than to test his happy memories against the litmus of time. For the period that followed was hardly conducive to nostalgia. In 1935, Nina Vidal divorced her husband and shortly thereafter married Hugh D. Auchincloss.[2] By 1936 her son was ensconced at Merrywood, the Auchincloss estate on the banks of the Potomac, which the author remembers today as a "political salon" where he met Dean Acheson and Arthur Krock among other notables.

A childhood like Gore Vidal's must, as T. S. Eliot's old magus said of his own journey to Bethlehem, be "set down." The medium must be fiction, which can refine the raw material of biography and provide the perfect buffer between the author and his life. Transparent names, telescoped events, and inverted chronology can create a part-dream, part-real world where family quarrels that ordinarily sputter out in half-finished recriminations can achieve the literacy of stichomythia, and where the family can become a Platonic reincarnation of its imperfect self. The Giraud of *The Season of Comfort* were one of these families—otherworldly enough to be archetypal, recognizable enough to be Vidal's, and neurotic enough to provide the scenario for an MGM dynasty movie.

During the forties, Vidal was writing verse to "kill off" the Hemingway influence and find a style that lay somewhere between the national manner and the national poetics.[3] He had been studying Rimbaud and Baudelaire; appropriately enough, the epigraph to *The Season of Comfort*, which Vidal began in March 1947, was from Rimbaud's *Une Saison en Enfer*. He retained the French, and there was no translation for the untutored. Like Rimbaud, Vidal also saw *l'enfer des femmes*, the women's hell; and like the questers of epic, he made his descent into that hell so that he could better understand life.

The novel opens in mid-June 1927, on the Hawkins' Virginia estate, with the birth of a son to Charlotte and Stephen Giraud. Charlotte's mother was a Governor's daughter, and her father was Senator Hawkins, a former Vice President, who denounced Franklin Delano Roosevelt as vehemently as Senator Gore did in real life. Charlotte was a debutante, but her husband had only "a good New Orleans name."

Obviously there is not the one-to-one ratio between the Giraud and the Vidals that the literalist is seeking. Gore Vidal was born in October 1925, not in June 1927; and in the Cadet Hospital at West Point, not on a Virginia estate. Senator Gore was not an ex-Vice President like Hawkins. On the other hand, "a good New Orleans name" like Giraud is a fairly close approximation of a venerable Venetian name like Vidal. The differences are hardly overwhelming; the facts are embellished, but their tenor is correct. Furthermore, there was something about Vidal's boyhood in Rock Creek Park and at Merrywood that suggested Senator Hawkins' world of good-natured black servants, cigar smoke, and political discussions on the veranda.

If fiction like *Gone with the Wind* (1936) or films like *Jezebel* (1938) are any indication, a novel about a Southern aristocracy should have its Scarlett O'Hara or Julie Marsden, clichés beatified as archetypes. The daughter of a former Vice President, while a sister to these grand ladies, cannot wreak havoc by mere eyelash-fluttering. She must function within the tradition established by the popular novel and the family dynasty film.

There was never a Southern belle like Charlotte Hawkins Giraud; she is Mrs. Morel and Regina Giddens, the bitch who suckles neither wisely nor well. She is also Fanny Skeffington, Bette Davis' most flamboyant creation (*Mr. Skeffington*, 1944); Fanny was sexually attracted to her brother Trippy who died in World War I. Charlotte Giraud also had a fanatical devotion to her brother William who was neither intelligent nor interesting; but he did write his sister misspelled letters which she idealized into models of epistolography. To her he was not William Hawkins, but "Clive Manners," the ultimate in cinematic nomenclature. His bedroom, which she would stealthily enter in his absence, was Valhalla, and his cap a Tarnhelm that made the wearer immune to reality. Naturally when William was killed in World War I,

Charlotte perpetuated his memory by naming her son after him.

At an early age Charlotte discovered that "the God her mother had taught her to pray to and sing about in the unpleasant dark church at home was, in reality, her father who sat on a throne."[4] After she erected her tabernacle to the divinized male, she went on to court the Muse of Tragedy. Aspiring to be an actress, Charlotte descended upon New York, where she met Stephen Giraud, a painter and frustrated politician. Both of them came from families that were religiously polarized. Charlotte's father was an agnostic, and her mother a staunch believer. Mrs. Giraud was a devout Catholic, but her son was not. Charlotte tried to legitimatize her neurosis in the theatre, and Stephen sought in politics the excitement he could never find in art. They were, as the film title says, made for each other.

And it was precisely the film that dictated the form of *The Season of Comfort*. Gore Vidal readily admits he is an inveterate moviegoer: "I saw every film Universal ever made during the forties, every Donald O'Connor and Peggy Ryan musical." But his viewing was not restricted to Universal's B movies; he obviously knew the finer products of Warner Brothers and especially MGM, to which Myra made a pilgrimage in the hope of finding the remains of Andy Hardy's house. Tell Vidal there is a revival of *Gilda* (1946) in midtown and he'll roll off the credits as rapidly as Myra named the cast of *The Uninvited* (1944) on her hospital bed: "Glenn Ford . . . Rita Hayworth . . . produced by Virginia Van Upp." He sighs, half nostalgically, half parodically: " 'Put the Blame on Mame, Boys.' I saw it; I saw them *all*."

While reading *The Season of Comfort*, one can taste the

déjà vu sticking to the palate like the topping from a marshmallow sundae. It conjures up the soda fountain, the forum where teen-agers assembled to debate the superiority of Tom Drake to Robert Walker. It becomes one of memory's corridors that suddenly expands into a movie theatre playing a triple bill of *The White Cliffs of Dover* (1944), *Wilson* (1944), and *The Green Years* (1946). After entering the theatre, one discovers that someone has edited the three films into one perfectly intelligible, full-length feature. And in a sense they all were the same film; while seemingly different, they worked from the same premises from which *The Season of Comfort* derives —a sensibility that was not too rarefied; diction slightly superior to the vernacular but not too erudite; neuroses that the unknowing would interpret as eccentricities; the collapsing of time into units of maturity and the reduction of character to stages of development; the *ab ovo–ad terminum*, sunrise-sunset cycle, or in the case of *The Season of Comfort*, the progression from Chapter One to Chapter Seven, both of which are entitled "The Beginning."

Since *The Season of Comfort* reproduces many of the Hollywood commonplaces, it achieves the verisimilitude of film, if not necessarily of fiction. One accepts Bill Giraud as the prototypical male extricating himself from his mother's coils in the same way one accepted Bette Davis in *Now Voyager* (1942) as the oppressed daughter of a Boston matriarch. In both cases, the characterizations conformed to what everyone knew, actually or intuitively, about children dominated by possessive mothers. Charlotte Hawkins Giraud is Terry Randall of *Stage Door*, leaving her socialite family to become an actress; Charlotte Vale of *Now Voyager* confronting her tyrannical mother; Fanny Skeffington grieving for a dead brother or descending a staircase thronged by suitors. She is any woman who was ever denied her first party, any socialite who married beneath herself, any mother who named her son after the brother she desired incestuously. In short, Charlotte is a reality and a cliché.

Structurally, *The Season of Comfort* harks back to movieland's halcyon days of the fade and the dissolve. Charlotte's entrance at a party triggers a memory of the one she never attended; and Bill's search for a funeral wreath occasions an extended reminiscence on his boyhood. One keeps recalling films like *And Now Tomorrow* (1944) where Emily Blair (Loretta Young), knowing she is incurably deaf, gazes despondently out of a train window. The glass becomes the reflector of the past, brightening gradually until it reveals the ballroom where her hearing suddenly ceased. Dissolve to a bed where she realizes the agony of a soundless world. Fade out and in to the lady sitting pensively in the train. Present-past-present: the cycle of the eternal return and indeed the cycle of *The Season of Comfort.*

In Chapter One, Charlotte is waiting to make her entrance at her son's christening. "It had been such a long time since her first party, the one she'd never gone to. She was fourteen then . . ." (p. 35). Fade in to the interior of Senator Hawkins' study in 1917, where Charlotte, on the eve of her first party, lashed out at her mother, accusing her of being an alcoholic. In retaliation, Clara Hawkins forbade her daughter to attend the party and confiscated her white dress. Lap dissolve and medium long shot of Charlotte, fourteen years later, resplendent at the christening in a white dress.

Chapter Three ("The White Flowers") ingeniously

cuts back and forth in time. At his grandfather's funeral, Bill is sent to fetch a wreath of calla lilies from a car. On his way to the parking lot, he is whisked back to his grammar school days of the *Arabian Nights* and the endless arguments with Senator Hawkins about the New Deal and Franklin D. Roosevelt, "the new President who couldn't walk." Cut to the driveway where the newsmen covering the funeral repeat the old stories about the mutual enmity between Hawkins and Roosevelt as if they had overheard Bill's reverie.

"Where *was* the car?" The car . . . the flowers. Iris shot of a bowl of yellow chrysanthemums for Bill's tenth birthday. Camp Sequence: camera pans bored faces of the boys while a counselor denounces Horatio Alger books because of their materialism and lectures on the wet dreams no one seemed to be having. Montage: Bill at twelve; his parents' divorce; the trip to Reno with Charlotte; the Washington, D.C., boarding school; his stepfather Roger Gilray; and his first love, Jimmy Wesson. Cut from love between two males to sex between male and female, Roger and Charlotte. Off-camera voices announce Charlotte's pregnancy. Close-up of Senator Hawkins extolling large families and unlimited life. Slow dissolve to the parking lot where the intimations of mortality propel Bill to the present and the matter at hand—the calla lilies which he finds and places on the coffin.

With Chapter Four, the flashbacks become less frequent. Instead there is a rapid, almost kaleidoscopic summary of Bill Giraud's life from fifteen to eighteen. Like his father, Bill discovered art, a medium the young Vidal also dabbled in, although he was a better sculptor than a painter. And like many prep school lads, he underwent the obligatory initiation into heterosexuality via the gang bang with a local whore, met a girl who understood his interest in art, severed mother's silver cord, was graduated, and enlisted in the army.

The Season of Comfort ends in the spring of 1945 with Bill's discovery that Jimmy Wesson was killed in action in the Pacific. A novel that begins with birth should end with death and rebirth, especially one that revolves about seasonal decay and renewal. All the formative influences of Bill's youth—Senator Hawkins, Charlotte and Stephen Giraud, Jimmy Wesson and Kay—pass out of sight, never really annihilated but never as operative as they once were. The phoenix dies and from his ashes the artist emerges. Stereotypy? Perhaps, yet one can only scale the ladder of perfection by leaving the lower rungs behind. Like his creator, Bill Giraud renounces the past and embraces the solitary life.

As cinema, *The Season of Comfort* is superb; as a novel, it is a series of literary commonplaces that are never noticed in the typical *Bildungsroman* because they are lost in the interstices of a symbolic structure. But *The Season of Comfort* is atypical; there is no symbolic structure, only a filmic one. The Rimbaud epigraph is a point of departure, not a controlling motif; the seasonal changes and colors are merely the passing of time. As autobiographical literature, *The Season of Comfort* lacks the final act of absolution for the parents whose sins were visited on their children.

Yet one should be kind to such novels. Certainly they afford greater pleasure than psycholinguistic exercises; but what stands in the way of total endorsement is their air of slickness, the glossy surface that is so transparent the reader not only sees himself (which is always the desideratum) but also all the archetypes behind the characters' faces. It isn't necessary to know about Jung to realize one is in the presence of an archetypal family, with its Sage-Father, Princess-Daughter, Suitor in quest of the Anima, and Child-Hero son. The movies had already reduced Freud to a series of complexes and Jung to a catechism of clichés. Everyone in *The Season of Comfort* has his Platonic form in so-called serious literature and his lower form in the movies. And so the novel lies somewhere in between.

For all its cinematic cleverness and a sentiment that smells of floral cutouts in a scrapbook, *The Season of Comfort*, like the novels that preceded it, has failed to provide even a preliminary sketch for a portrait of the author. Bill Giraud resembles the negative of a lost snapshot; Vidal has deliberately darkened aspects of his character that should have been illuminated and brightened what should have remained in shadow.

Gore Vidal wanted himself to be known, but not wholly. He would not wear his heart on his sleeve for daws to peck at. A true son of the Classics, he saw the cult of emotion as democracy's revenge on the individual—a cult which, if not checked, would subvert privacy and reduce everyone to a known quantity:

I suppose there are some who say of others pejoratively, "His feelings are not deep." But if pressed, they would admit that no one really knows what another's feelings are.... In any case ... feeling is all, and the deliberate exercise of mind is thought an admission of emotional poverty.[5]

—"Love Love Love" (1959)

Gore Vidal would undoubtedly endorse what T. S. Eliot said of the depersonalized poet in "Tradition and the Individual Talent": "Only those who have personality and emotions know what it means to want to escape from these things."

4

The Entertainer

By 1950 GORE VIDAL had acquired the reputation of being the most prolific of the postwar novelists. Within a five-year period he had published *Williwaw* (1946), *In a Yellow Wood* (1947), *The City and the Pillar* (1948), *The Season of Comfort* (1949), *A Search for the King* (1950), and *Dark Green, Bright Red* (1950)—a feat literary historians of the next century might ponder as they record the palmy days of Iris Murdoch, a similarly prodigious writer who contributed almost a novel a year to the Age of Aquarius.

Since Vidal was producing so rapidly, it was inevitable that Dutton would space the publication of his novels. Their decision was understandable; Vidal had completed *The City and the Pillar* before *In a Yellow Wood* was even in galleys, and had begun *A Search for the King* in November 1947, shortly after finishing *The Season of Com-*

fort. A novel a year was the publishers' desideratum; it was also the golden mean between familiarity that breeds contempt and oblivion that yields no royalties.

But the idea of bringing out *A Search for the King* and *Dark Green, Bright Red* within ten months of each other did not prove especially felicitous. Readers simply did not associate Vidal with the historical romance and the espionage tale, which were new genres for him. To most readers, he was the postwar *Wunderkind* of *Williwaw* who turned postwar profligate with *The City and the Pillar*; but another Thomas B. Costain or Eric Ambler he was not.

"My two novels were entertainments," Vidal insists. "They were invented, totally made up. But nobody at the time wanted a skillfully told story. It was the same with *Weekend*. Who cared about a quiet comedy?" Apparently only a few, for in 1968 it lasted a little more than two weeks on Broadway; and at mid-century only a few could accept a historical novel where the women were insignificant, and a tale of revolution where the men were idle dreamers.

When an author follows an autobiographical novel with a historical romance, one is tempted to regard it as a *divertissement* or a respite from soul-baring. But Vidal never unknotted the cord of his life; in *The Season of Comfort* he only loosened some of the nodes. While *A Search for the King* was hardly a probing of the past, it was a return to the author's boyhood—to the attic library in Senator Gore's Rock Creek Park home where Vidal ruined his eyes reading the *Congressional Record* for his grandfather's edification and *The Book of Knowledge* for his own.

As a boy, Vidal was attracted to the story of Richard the Lion-Hearted and his troubadour Blondel; as a man he decided to write a novel about it. Although *A Search for the King* was an entertainment, it still manifested Jim Willard's quest for a world elsewhere in which devotion between men could have a sacramental character. This theme haunts the novel like some plaintive folk motif in Bartók where the race suffers with a musical purity the *Volksgeist* could never comprehend. Loss, love, the affection of an older man for a boy, and obligatory sex with females that mocks the undemanding camaraderie of males are all part of *A Search for the King*. Vidal merely transferred his earlier preoccupations to the twelfth century.

While *A Search for the King* will always be considered one of Vidal's minor efforts, one can respect the author's attempt to inject some art into the tired formula for historical fiction; and a formula is precisely what most contemporary novelists of this school employ. Take an era like the Middle Ages; define it in terms familiar to those who learned about the Crusades from Cecil B. De Mille and about Robin Hood from Errol Flynn. Select a speech pattern somewhere between the vernacular and the archaic; call it Twentieth-Century Quaint. Have characters indulge in molten love-making *à la* Frank Yerby where a woman's conical breasts are always stabbing her lover's chest with their "firepoints." And by all means, stamp every page with the watermark of living history by using (sparingly) key words like "hauberk," "bliaut," and "paynim." The reader need not know what they mean as long as they sound medieval.

Vidal's only concession to the formula is the dialogue, which attests to his familiarity with Universal's *oeuvre*, particularly films like *Arabian Nights* (1942) and *Ali Baba and the Forty Thieves* (1943). When the disguised Richard senses danger, he delivers his instructions like a stone-faced Jon Hall: " 'Baudoin, William, Blondel and I will travel together. The rest of you must find your way back as best you can. Present yourselves to me in London when you arrive and I shall remember you. Now separate. In God's name.' "[1]

Most historical novelists never convince the educated reader they have researched their subject. Vidal does, and he offers more than a bookish allusion or a hint of documentation for the scholars who must justify their bedtime reading. Vidal knew that the lover in Troubadour poetry served the Lady the same way the vassal served his lord:

For the Lady was many things. . . . The Lady was the comradeship of knights. The Lady was beauty. The Lady was the mother of God. So she stood as a symbol for many things, for all the passion and all the beauty in the world. (p. 51)

Vidal also knew how the Lady was addressed; she was called *"midons,"* "my lord," not "my lady," in what Leslie Fiedler termed "the natural language of subordination." Furthermore, the author, who claimed descent from the troubadour Vidal, had read enough Courtly Love lyrics to realize that while these poems seemed pure of heart and imitative of the *Ave Maria*, they actually reflected the poet's hope of committing adultery with the lady of the manor.

By selecting twelfth-century Western Europe as a potential Utopia for males in quest of pure comradeship, Vidal has again anticipated Leslie Fiedler's *Love and Death in the American Novel*. Fiedler began his inquiry into the origins of sentimental love with the Middle

Ages, when the Lady, the White Goddess masquerading as the Virgin Mary, reduced her male devotees to whining melancholics. While the American wilderness novel with its unsuspecting homoerotics seemed eons removed from Courtly Love poetry with its manly knights, Fiedler saw a connection between them. Both stood in awe of the Great Mother; both merged into homosexuality:

If on the one hand the code of courtly love blurs oddly into heresy . . . on the other, it even more strangely merges with homosexuality. Indeed, one senses from the start in the verse of courtly love a desire to mitigate by ritualized and elegant foreplay a final consummation felt as brutal, or else a desire to avoid entirely any degrading conjunction with female flesh.[2]

Although *A Search for the King* appeared a decade before *Love and Death in the American Novel,* Vidal came to the same conclusions in fiction that Fiedler reached in criticism. In fact, *A Search for the King* is a perfect illustration of Fiedler's thesis about Courtly Love. Naturally Richard's troubadour would seek a boy's devotion after years of prostrating himself before the Lady. Calling a woman "my lord" for too long can blur all sexual distinctions.

Behind the Courtly Love ballads, with their endearing conventions, was a theology of marriage which Vidal understood thoroughly. When Blondel encounters a monk, the conversation turns to marriage. Brother Antonio champions what C. S. Lewis in *The Allegory of Love* called "the 'sexology' of the medieval church": " 'Procreation can be accomplished without lust. . . . It should be performed as a sacred duty rather than as a source of pleasure—the motive, unhappily, of most people' " (p. 170).

The monk's warped concept of sex has left its mark on the troubadour. If love between man and woman is merely flesh against flesh, Blondel wonders whether the whole Courtly Love tradition is not fraudulent. Perhaps the lyrics he sang were only "the debris of loving," meaningless formulae threaded into pearls of poetry. No doubt the twelfth-century poet faced a similar dilemma, wondering where genuine emotion began and metaphor ended.

Vidal also differed from other practitioners of historical fiction by his approach to Richard the Lion-Hearted, whom most novelists would have made the central character. But the King was merely another amorphous male in the tradition of John Martin–Robert Holton–Jim Willard–Bill Giraud. If not Richard, then his brother John or his mother Eleanor would qualify. While they appear, their contribution is negligible. John is the villain of melodrama, and Eleanor is an aging matriarch. The novel is about Richard's troubadour, Blondel de Néel, and his need to possess in a male the perfection of love he ascribed to the female. It is as if one were to rewrite *Don Quixote*, making Sancho the hero and consigning the Don to a secondary role.

Blondel undergoes the usual trials of the faithful servant in search of his king. He soothes semiliterate Normans with a love poem at an inn, tangles with Hedwig of Tierstein, a *donna* who is hardly a lady, seduces a peasant girl, encounters a band of werewolves who are nothing more than thieves in wolves' clothing, and barely escapes a luncheon with a giant who cannibalizes boys. Finally Blondel meets his own adoring youth, Karl, and with this love comes a reversal of roles. It is Blondel who is the beloved, and Karl who is the lover.

After years of vassalage, Blondel is now the object of veneration. He is *"midons."*

In his delicate handling of the bond between the boy and the troubadour, Vidal the classicist overcomes Vidal the medievalist. Blondel and Karl do not suggest Roland and Oliver as much as they do Achilles and Patroclus. Vidal obviously prefers the *Iliad* to the *Song of Roland.*

Karl was earmarked for destruction the moment he first approached Blondel and inquired breathlessly about the military life and the troubadour's vocation. Like Patroclus, Karl yearned for the *kudos* only battle could bring. The brief time Blondel spent with the boy recalls the halcyon days of Achilles and Patroclus—afternoons of silent camaraderie and evenings with the girls from the court.

This was also Achilles' world, as Homer described it in the *Iliad.* The silence of the tent he shared with Patroclus was broken only by the songs they sang of heroes. At night, each slept with a woman by his side. The bisexual goal? If so, it was only realizable in the Heroic Age where gender and sex were not synonyms.

Patroclus demanded his *aristeia,* which led to his death at the hands of Hector. Karl also sought his moment of glory and was slain in battle. When Achilles learned of his friend's death, he began a threnody that reached the depths of the sea. But Blondel is a Homeric type, not a Homeric hero. There is no lamentation; Blondel is too shattered by the day's events to exhibit grief. As he cradles the boy in his arms, a spring rain falls, and with it comes the knowledge that his youth ended with Karl's death.

Again Vidal has argued that human relationships of any kind and in any era are sadly ephemeral. Within the deceptively unphilosophical framework of the romance, he wrote his *envoi* to love; but he also reworked a boyhood story about a troubadour's search for a king into a poet's search for a union he could never find with the women he serenaded and laid.

Dark Green, Bright Red was also more than a "skillfully told story." The novel reflects Vidal's vision of Guatemala, where he lived, on and off, between 1947 and 1949. It was never a popular book, although a few laudatory adjectives were culled from the reviews to form a provocative blurb. However, it was one of the author's more successful attempts to amalgamate film and fiction; Vidal shot Latin America in a combination of vivid Technicolor and aquatint–pastel houses in a rose-white town, jungle foliage so green it made the sunlight emerald, leaves as translucent as stained-glass windows.

The plot recalls a host of movies without resembling any specific one. On August 30, 1949, a group of the most diversified revolutionaries imaginable gathered in Tenango to restore the fallen dictator, General Alvarez, to the presidency of the Republic. *Mirabile dictu*, one of John Wayne's minor epics, *Tycoon* (1947), was set in Tenango, a half-name (e.g., Chimaltenango, Huehuetenango, Quezaltenango) so phonetically sensuous it could convince any audience it was as real as Pago Pago or Bombay.

In the best tradition of the Hollywood scenario, Alvarez is described so generally he could be Juan José Arévalo or Akim Tamiroff; he is merely a composite of popular opinion. His nineteen-year-old presidency of the Republic came to an abrupt end when he was overthrown in a student-supported coup led by Ospina, a leftist professor advocating agrarian reform. The situation is promising; no clash is more exciting than one between a Catholic (Alvarez) who has revolution in his blood because the founder of his religion was a "right-on" radical, and a Bolshevik (Ospina) to whom revolution is an article of ideology rather than of faith.

But this is a soundstage revolution that can never accomplish its goal because no one takes it seriously. The participants are contract players, loan-outs, featured actors, each of whom plays his role as if he had entrusted his meager ability to a minor director who, in turn, diminished what little talent was already there. The protagonist, if one can use the term, is Peter Nelson, a court-martialed West Pointer turned soldier of fortune for no explicable reason. He is twenty-six, the mean age of the male in the early novels, vaguely defined and uninteresting. Nelson is John Martin in a cadre, Robert Holton trying to be *engagé* in Latin America, Bill Giraud drilling natives because the script calls for it. Peter's goal is hardly the social betterment of the working class; he "wanted money" and in this respect his values scarcely differ from Holton's.

Then there are the General's children, José and Elena. José is the stereotyped Latin jealously guarding his sister's virtue from the excitable Nelson who, one knows, will possess her before the novel ends. For a Catholic, Elena is not exactly the sacrificial type. She prefers the cultural life of New Orleans, where the family spent two comfortable years in exile, to the artistic cloaca of Tenango. Her *engagement* is so disarmingly vapid that one can accept her only as a parody of an ingenue. She defends her father with the flighty logic of an English major who discovered her social conscience in Ethnic Studies 101: " 'Oh, but he wasn't a dictator! At least he wasn't like Hitler or Mussolini, not that kind at all. He was a very *special* kind of President. You see, since so few of the people read and write, people need somebody to look after them . . . somebody like Father.' "[3]

Every Latin American cadre should have an intellectual and a buffoon priest—the former for witty repartee, the latter for comic relief. The intellectual is Charles de Cluny, Noel Coward turned radical in middle age; de Cluny convinced himself he was a product of postwar disillusionment, renounced fiction, and became a speech writer for Alvarez. The priest is Father Miguel, an asthmatic with a blackhead-pitted nose who delivers panegyrics to Mother Church to justify his none-too-selfless role in the revolution. Let's not forget the Billie Burke type, Mrs. Eggleton, the wealthy American living in Tenango, gushing and scatterbrained. And at some point a living paradox should appear, to confirm the popular belief that revolutions are the last stronghold of heterogeneity. Enter an Oklahoma newspaperman whose burning ambition is to produce the definitive translation of Aristophanes' *The Birds*.

So much for the heroes. The villains are an enigmatic duo, Mr. Green and his nephew George, of the "Company." If one interprets the "Company" in the right way, the green-red symbolism becomes apparent: these were the colors of the original Ugly American, the United Fruit Company, which Pablo Neruda called "the dictatorship of the flies" in one of his poems. The Greens, who seemed to support the General's Catholic Socialist Party, were really in league with Ospina. Ospina gave Alvarez his brief gaudy hour because he knew the General would try to take the Republic by force and in so doing would expose himself as an anarchist. When the revolution collapses, the cast disperses, the flats are struck, and Peter Nelson leaves Tenango humming a popular song in another of Vidal's bluebird endings.

A revised *Dark Green, Bright Red*, of which Vidal is especially proud, came out a few months after the 1968 riots at Columbia and the Sorbonne. Measured against the revolutionary spirit of the late sixties, when the kids stepped into roles their elders were glad to relinquish and played out an unresolved scenario to its dénouement of ennui, *Dark Green, Bright Red* is more of a parody of revolution than a novel of or about it. Its cynicism, which is not tempered in the revision, underscores Vidal's point that no one is selfless enough to make the revolution work. Even Alvarez, anti-Commie that he is, argues for keeping up with the times: " 'The world is moving to the Left, my friends. I move with the world, just as the Republic must' " (p. 16).

Which side is anyone on? At times the novel seems to be more about a political convention than a takeover in a banana republic. Or perhaps there is no difference.

Dark Green, Bright Red is proof that Vidal "killed off" Hemingway and the telegraphic style. If the novel is a parody of revolution, then Peter Nelson of the wholesome name is a parody of the Hemingway hero. Exactly what the Ohio-born, ex-West Pointer is doing in Tenango is never explained. José Alvarez, an army buddy, invited him there, and having been court-martialed recently, Nelson accepted. Yet Nelson is totally uncommitted to the revolution or to anything. When he finally beds down with Elena, the pink and gold of the sky change to a sullen red as the two of them writhe with the frustration of novices aligning their bodies for intercourse. The unsatisfying attempt at sex is a metaphor for the revolution that was intended to unite men of varying backgrounds but only succeeded in separating them.

In the 1950 *Dark Green, Bright Red*, Vidal, who would later call himself a liberal Democrat, ridiculed political tags like "liberal" and "conservative"; in the 1968 revision, he darkened the so-called shades of meaning in "left" and "right" into shadows of confusion. When George Green tries to give Peter a clearer picture of General Alvarez's politics, he sounds like someone trying to explain the difference between William F. Buckley, Jr., and David Susskind:

George looked suddenly fierce. "They want this whole place to go Commie, and it will if they keep meddling. They don't realize that these people are much better off with somebody like Alvarez . . . than with a half-baked intellectual like Ospina who isn't even a proper Commie; he just dislikes Right-wingers, which makes him what they call a liberal."

"Confusing. So Alvarez is the Right—"

"But has to pretend he's Left."

"And Ospina's the Center—"

"But is really Left, but pink not red."

"Then who is the real Left?"

"What they call intellectuals." (p. 62)

Q. E. D.

5

A Sentimental Education

NINETEEN FORTY-EIGHT was Gore Vidal's *Wanderjahr*. He left his Guatemala retreat for a European sabbatical, traveling through Italy in a jeep with Tennessee Williams and visiting Santayana in the Convent of the Blue Nuns in Rome. In Paris, *le maître* André Gide presented him with a copy of *Corydon*, his famous dialogue on homosexuality, "as one prophet to another." At Cambridge, E. M. Forster welcomed him to his musty rooms, where he informed his young guest that he also had written a book in which two boys lounged about in bed extolling the virtues of male friendship; thus Vidal had heard about Forster's *Maurice* (1971) long before it was published posthumously in the tolerant seventies.

Nineteen forty-eight was also Vidal's *annus mirabilis*, a year he would recall with pleasure in *Two Sisters*. The

City and the Pillar, which he then considered his greatest
novel, was selling well; Christopher Isherwood called it
"one of the best novels of its kind," and Thomas Mann
wrote that Goer *(sic)* Vidal had produced "a noble
work." But more important, Vidal had moved from the
brownstone coteries of the West Village to the literary
salons of Europe. It was an experience that had to be
recorded in a novel of exquisite sensibility written in a
baronial setting where the appointments would complement the style.

The novel was *The Judgment of Paris* (1952), which appeared four years after the European odyssey. In the
interim, Vidal returned to Guatemala to finish *Dark
Green, Bright Red;* then, in the tradition of the movie
travelogues, he bid adieu to the rose-white towns and
emerald foliage, returned to New York, and in 1950
bought a house on the Hudson in Dutchess County.

Since the novels after *The City and the Pillar* were financial failures, the purchase of a mansion built in 1820 by
Governor Livingston of New York seemed somewhat
foolhardy. Yet Edgewater, a name Vidal found deplorably literal, was a necessity. Physically, the mansion with
its Greek columns resembled a hall of learning in a
Southern university town; it was the perfect site for the
college education the author never had. On the banks of
the Hudson, he assimilated all three volumes of George
Saintsbury's *A History of Criticism*, which influenced the
style of his essays, studied the eighteenth-century English novel, and developed a close kinship with Henry
James. Shakespeare's plays were absent from his reading
list, since he had read them under Senator Gore's men-
torship in Rock Creek Park. It was a crash major in
English Lit, and Vidal was graduated *summa cum laude*
from Edgewater.

One should be grateful to Edgewater U., where there were no classroom critics around dissecting literary cadavers and leaving them to rot. In another era, Vidal might have joined that tribe of academicians who write novels for their colleagues to teach. He has never fully accepted Academe for reasons that many professors would also accept; Vidal regards the scholars writing for the prestigious quarterlies as little more than "mechanics . . . dismantling the text with the same rapture their simpler brothers experience while taking apart combustion engines"[1]—as perfect a description of the New Criticism as one will ever find.

Vidal's poetics came from his reading, and in the essay-novel he found the model for his *Wanderjahr*. He envisioned a novel on the order of *Tom Jones* (1749) where a sensuous but decent lad journeyed through a world of seducers eager to ensnare him in their fine meshes. Vidal wanted the intimacy between narrator and reader that Fielding achieved in *Tom Jones*, in addition to a flexibility that could accommodate asides to the "good reader" and a sense of the bawdy that never went beyond a peep through the bedroom keyhole. It would be a deceptively episodic book whose three parts were connected by a theory of fiction evolving simultaneously with an aesthetic of love.

Stories about a guileless young man's initiation into the ways of the world tend to resemble one another because they are variations of the journey archetype in which the wayfarer/quester/youth from the country is buffeted by real or metaphorical waves. Likewise, fiction in which three temptresses appear at various stages of the journey strike the same archetypal chord. Odysseus almost fell in love with Nausicaä and was seduced by Circe and Calypso before his reunion with Penelope.

Tom Jones had his flings with Molly Seagrim, Mrs. Waters, and Lady Bellaston before marrying Sophia Western. Philip Warren will obviously follow a similar course.

The Judgment of Paris is a mythic novel that will evoke any *Bildungsroman*, every journey myth the preconscious psyche revealed, and every tale of a hero and his amours —three profane and one sacred—from the *Odyssey* to *Last of the Red Hot Lovers*. *Tom Jones* provided the basic situation for Vidal, and the rest is literally myth.

In classical mythology, Paris, the Trojan shepherd, was asked to judge the famous beauty contest between Hera, Athena, and Aphrodite. Hera tempted him with power, Athena with military success, and Aphrodite with Helen, the paragon of beauty. Paris awarded the prize to Aphrodite, and the Trojan War followed shortly thereafter.

Vidal saw a parallel between Paris, whose pastoral simplicity concealed an itching libido, and the equally guileless Tom Jones, whose sexual ethics were moderately hedonistic but by no means ungentlemanly: " 'I have been guilty with women, I own it; but am not conscious that I have ever injured any.' " Paris, Tom, and Vidal's hero, Philip Warren, never took the initiative in sex; the female was the predator, the male the prey. In fact, what Henry James said of Fielding's hero in the Preface to *The Princess Casamassima*, a novel Vidal knew intimately, applies to Warren as well; Tom may be a superb example of comic bewilderment but he "hasn't a grain of imagination."

Philip Warren planted his solitary grain of imagination in a projected novel that yielded one short paragraph about a woman who communicated on pale blue stationery because of a childhood indignity in a Grand Central Station phone booth. He realizes the story will lead nowhere. It has only the rhythm of high comedy, produced not by wit but by the incongruity of a girl's being molested in a phone booth while her mother was buying a ticket to Peekskill. It is the kind of writing that is cut to the contours of the author's pumpkin grin.

Although Philip abandoned his first attempt at fiction, the one paragraph of a supposedly never-to-be-finished novel became a metaphor for the novel itself. *The Judgment of Paris* is an enlargement of that eccentric and incongruous opening; it is a novel where portentous plots collapse when the conspirators lose interest in them, women beckon mysteriously from the shadows of the Coliseum, and young men bear their chalice (occasionally dropping it) through a crowd of infidels.

Philip Warren was twenty-eight. A navy man and a Harvard Law School graduate, he has come to Europe for that mythical year of self-discovery. At first there is the shudder of recognition: *In a Yellow Wood* again, the road not taken, the *donna* who philosophizes between her legs. To some extent the shudder is justified; the lady of theory ruined *In a Yellow Wood*, and she may return to play havoc with *The Judgment of Paris*. Three ladies appear in the novel as the modern incarnations of Hera, Athena, and Aphrodite; but they can no more alter the course of the plot than they could the myth from which they came. Vidal exorcised the White Goddess before she entered his soul; he locked her in myth where she belonged.

Vidal has tempered his misogyny by using a voice that describes and comments with the same dry neutrality. Philip no sooner checks into his hotel than the author's voice queries his creation: "Now then: what does he look like? What sort of man or boy or youth is Philip Warren?"[2] The portrait that follows is pure Fielding, whose descriptions are either elaborate catalogues of externals (and therefore not descriptions of character at all) or chalk outlines the reader must fill in. Sophia Western is depicted in such lush detail that the colors cancel each other out as they splash pell-mell on the canvas: nicely proportioned arms, symmetrical limbs, hair falling in graceful curls, arched eyebrows, oval cheeks, a finely turned neck. "Such was the outside of Sophia." And such, one might add, was any virginal heroine's. Yet in introducing Partridge, Fielding simply informs the reader that he has certain peculiarities that will not be mentioned "as the reader will himself very easily perceive them on his farther acquaintance with this extraordinary person."

Vidal combines both methods in his description of the hero. At first he shrugs and entrusts Philip to nature, which is always the best revealer of character: "Well, it is much too early to draw any conclusions about his character since he is hardly yet revealed." Thereupon he catalogues everything connected with Philip's outside, from his oval cheeks to the butterfly tattoo on his left thigh.

In Rome, Philip falls into adventures as easily as Tom fell into the bushes. He becomes a courier for a homosexual coterie attempting to restore the House of Savoy. Philip enters the conspiracy like the bumpkin hero of the movies who blundered into the underworld, blissfully unaware of danger and eager to perform any action that would give his flat character a third dimension. In addition to being inexperienced, Philip is, as one soon discovers, loveless. Therefore he will embrace any group that promises camaraderie, even if its members are more oriented toward Turkish baths than revolutions. Philip Warren is Tom Jones embroiled in gay intrigue, relishing the peril but discreetly disassociating himself from the conspirators' sexual persuasion.

But the modern Tom is pursued by tempters of both sexes. At nightfall in the Coliseum, Philip's reverie on mortality is interrupted by a throaty voice asking whether the ruins of Madison Square Garden will ever be as impressive as the Roman rubble. The voice belongs to Regina Durham, a modern Hera; her husband is appropriately named Rex, Zeus incarnate as a powerful congressman and presidential adviser. Just as Hera bribed Paris with power, Regina tempts Philip with the offer of a political career, which he declines. But he does not decline the offer of her body, and their liaison at the Excelsior Hotel gives the narrator a chance to invade the privacy of the boudoir for a discourse on the role of sex in literature.

The model is again Fielding, who devoted the prefatory chapter of Book II of *Tom Jones* to a digression on the nature of history. Vidal chose to muse on sex: Should lovers in a novel hear the music of the spheres or the creaking of the springs? The author opts for classic sex, not the nitty-gritty. The description of the scene becomes The Scene—copulation by wit. There is no more sexuality in the digression than there was in the act. Each is a literary device working within a literary novel.

After the obligatory love scene has been played and analyzed, Vidal returns to the plot, which is more or less the education of Philip Warren. Since the hero's only personality is the adjectival façade the author gave him, he assumes whatever role fortune offers him at the moment. At present it is courier for the bogus conspirators, Clyde Norman and Lord Glenellen. Philip dashes off to Amalfi with a cryptic message no one is interested in receiving. When he returns to Rome, he discovers that the revolutionaries have tired of their game and Lord Glenellen has become a Communist.

The post-Hiroshima generation Vidal is depicting in *The Judgment of Paris* is, existentially at any rate, more suited to satire than the expatriates of the 1920's. It was a generation that embraced mysticism with the first fervor of a novice, worshiping the alien and the exotic. Regina predicts a return to primitivism, with the forces of nature replacing crucified saviors and virgin mothers. "You cannot cheat the dark gods," Honor Klein warned in Iris Murdoch's *A Severed Head* (1961). It is the dark gods, too long ignored, who will return; and with them, the new messiah.

Regina basks in the twilight of Christianity like a philosophy student who just discovered Nietzsche. Norman and Glenellen are textbook radicals; when one book on revolution loses its appeal, they exchange it for another in a different series. Philip watches all of them playact through life, making and retracting portentous statements, changing ideologies as often as empires altered their boundaries. He is being educated into a diluted existentialism where actions are important only to the degree that one invests them with meaning. What is so hilarious and at the same time deplorable about these pseudo-existentialists is the fact that they invest their actions with no meaning at all.

Each of the three parts of *The Judgment of Paris* revolves

about a major cultural center and its tutelary goddess: Rome as a seat of political power (Regina/Hera), Egypt as a source of mysterious knowledge (Sophia/Athena), and Paris as the locale of *grand amour* (Anna/Aphrodite). Vidal explodes each myth by reducing the centers to guidebook stereotypes and the goddesses to fraudulent *femmes fatales.* Regina promises Philip a career in politics, but how she can effect it is never clarified. Mythic creations have their own *raison d'être,* which one does not question. As Queen of Heaven and consort of the Sky God, she should have the solution to the riddle of the cosmos; yet she speaks in riddles herself about the agon between the hanged gods and their usurpers.

Philip tries to penetrate the inscrutable mysteries of Egypt through Sophia, the Athena figure who offers him the wisdom her name implies. Philip has only intellectual commerce with her; sex with Wisdom is an abstraction only a metaphysician can contemplate. Sophia has the look of the Sibyl in her eyes, but she is enslaved to a prophet who foretells the coming of a messiah. When she requests further information about the savior who will dispel man's fear of death, the prophet rises abruptly and terminates the audience. The oracles are silent or cheat. Sophia, like Regina, was a fraud. She was searching for knowledge herself, devoting her time to interrogating mystics whose art of equivocation could not withstand analysis. Rome and Regina, Egypt and Sophia have failed the hero. One more goddess remains: Aphrodite, whom Philip encounters in Egypt but possesses in Paris.

Initially, Parts I and II, Rome and Egypt, seem unrelated, but they are linked by a common motif—the plot that will turn the detached Philip Warren into *l'homme engagé.* In Rome he became a messenger for a pair of mad

Englishmen; in Egypt he agrees to procure poison for the elephantine Mr. Willys who is anxious to shuffle off his mortal coil. In each case, Philip's first reaction was to hurl himself into the plot; any sort of commitment or lunatic scheme was preferable to nothingness. But he reneged, and the task was entrusted to Fay Peabody, a detective writer, who bungled her first two attempts. Willys finally got his wish and died from a heart attack.

At first, one suspects Vidal of indulging in madcap comedy for its own sake by introducing a hairbrained novelist who cannot put her theory of homicide into practice. Yet *The Judgment of Paris* is, among other things, a fiction about the writing of fiction, where the author is experimenting with different forms—the picaresque, the mythic, the *Bildungsroman,* and the essay-novel. In Part II, Vidal parodies the *roman policier* and the rationalism it promotes. Where is intricate plotting better found than in the detective story? Mrs. Peabody's theory of fiction is based on personal experience as opposed to "faulty verisimilitude." If there is one hallowed element of fiction absent in *The Judgment of Paris,* it is verisimilitude. Characters arrive and depart with the most tenuous motivation, and scenes change like projections on a cyclorama. As a further extension of the literary *jeu,* characters from Vidal's other novels pop up with additions to their résumés: Robert Holton of *In a Yellow Wood* has taken a position with the State Department; Charles de Cluny of *Dark Green, Bright Red* has become a courtier without a court; and Jim Willard of *The City and the Pillar* is hustling in Paris.

The Judgment of Paris is not only an exercise in the craft of fiction but also a retrospective of the author's earlier work. If Vidal is parodying the conventions of the novel, he is also parodying himself. The devices he mocks are those he once took seriously—the solipsistic male, the hero pursued by seducers of both sexes, the sirens with their songs of love, the "faulty verisimilitude" of an American embroiled in a plot he does not even understand. *The Judgment of Paris* is Vidal's *Candide* as well as his *Tom Jones*—an elaborate spoof of the mimetic mind that deduces its rules for art from an optimistic belief in order.

Philip's last stop is Paris, where Glenellen and Norman reappear like Dr. Pangloss and Cunegonde. They have attached themselves to a hermaphrodite, Augustus /Augusta, and now officiate at its *levée*. The hermaphrodite is merely another diversion as they pass time waiting for a deliverer. The episode is Vidal's *reductio ad absurdum* of the religious renewal in the 1950's, a theme he will explore in greater depth in *Messiah*. The fear of another war produced such a climate of superstition that the misguided clutched at anything resembling the messianic—Billy Graham for the believers, hermaphrodites for the agnostics. And when no messiah was forthcoming, they invented their own.

In Paris, Anna/Aphrodite supervises the final stage of Philip's education. The narrative voice that guided him through the rubrics of sweatless sex with Regina intrudes once more to witness his penetration of Anna. The setting is ideal—a seascape of crying gulls and breakers crashing on the sand. But when Philip is on the verge of becoming a man of flesh and sinews, the narrator interrupts to remind us that sex is the proper collocation of adjectives and not the conjugation of bodies.

At the end of the novel, Philip must choose between the three goddesses. The reviewers claimed he selected

Anna, but Vidal will only say that the hero chose Love. The conclusion was intentionally ambiguous. As Philip turns to address Sophia, she suddenly withdraws into the shadows, and a marble figure falls to the ground. Wisdom has shattered, but beyond the pieces an apparition materializes—a Madonna in a grotto of seaweed and mother-of-pearl. It is not Anna Morris as she was, but Anna transfigured. The real Anna was a goddess *manquée*, a Spider Woman in gossamer dangling at the center of her web. The transfigured Anna is the Star of the Sea, an *objet d'art* framed by pearl and seaweed. To enter this womb of shell, Philip must strip off his flesh and metamorphose into an art object himself. "Love Love Love," Vidal's recurrent theme and constant lament, is possible only through a transformation that requires the total surrender of one's humanity to art.

Even the transfigured Anna will not satisfy Philip. Beyond her lies another, "a dreaming figure" who stirs and opens her golden eyes. What Philip ultimately desires is the archetype behind the transformation, the pure anima. He experiences something similar to what William Gaddis described in his novel, *The Recognitions* (1955): a forged Titian is scraped away; beneath it lies a worthless original, and under that, a priceless masterpiece.

In the ending, Vidal parts company with all of his influences. It is true that Fielding was also preoccupied with love in *Tom Jones* and devoted the prefatory chapter of Book VI to proving it was the highest form of bliss for the naturally good. Vidal would concur, but only if the statement read: "the highest form of bliss for the mythically good." Physical love, even when practiced by men and women of good nature, is much too messy. Thus

Vidal poeticizes it to justify its existence in both life and literature.

Wondrous to say, "Love Love Love" is possible in the Vidal canon. But one must be disembodied to achieve it.

6

Manchild in the Media

AMONG the editions in the Vidal Collection at Madison is an "Edgar Box" mystery novel, *Death in the Fifth Position.* Inscribed on the title page, in Vidal's unmistakable penmanship, is a brief apologia: "This was written in seven days, a chapter a day, to survive in 1951."

Compared to the *annus mirabilis* of 1948, 1951 was the year of the locust. To preserve his temple on the Hudson and his integrity as well, Vidal began writing thrillers under the pseudonym of Edgar Box. Although the books were intentionally lurid, they contained enough references to HUAC, the arts, and politics to qualify for that intermediate stage between Grand Guignol and tripe. The Edgar Box hero was ex-drama critic Peter Cutler Sargeant III, the sophisticate's answer to Mike Hammer. Sargeant did not cover the waterfront, but was more comfortable tangling with a Commie choreographer *(Death in the Fifth Position,* 1952), investigating the murder of a presidential candidate with the aristocratic name of Leander Rhodes *(Death before Bedtime,* 1953), and solving a throat-cutting at an Easthampton estate *(Death Likes It Hot,* 1954).

At first the identity of Edgar Box eluded most of the reviewers, some of whom even found him "gifted" and the successor to Dashiell Hammett and Raymond Chandler. But by 1954, Edgar Box had been unmasked; Frank Farrell, a columnist for the New York *World-Telegram,* noted in his usual subway style, terse and packed, that Gore Vidal "swaps grandiloquence for faster loot in penning hit whodunits under that Edgar Box alias."

In addition to making some fast loot, Vidal can look back on the survival years with the same amusement I. A. Richards must have experienced when he assigned his students poems for evaluation without revealing their authorship. Just as Richards discovered that one of John Donne's *Holy Sonnets* was the work of "a very simple man," Vidal found that Edgar Box ran the gamut from an author who "handles sex with a racy good humor that reminds the reader of the lusty boys of Shakespeare's day" to a purveyor of "trash." The British also welcomed Edgar Box, and the *Times Literary Supplement* reviewer gave a favorable notice to *Death in the Fifth Position,* although he was distressed by the graphic description of a burned corpse.

The thrillers compensated for the financial failure of *The Judgment of Paris* (1952) and *Messiah* (1954); they also paid for the maintenance of Edgewater. But Edgar Box was not the answer for Gore Vidal, who made a twofold discovery in "the black winter of 1953": the novel as a popular art form had been interred, and with it the post-war prodigy who once published six novels in five years. Vidal has exaggerated his premature demise in the early fifties; he was not mentioned in the past tense as often as he thought. In regard to his frequent obituaries for the novel, Vidal insists he really meant fiction had lost its audience to television, a belief he reiterated in his 1972 hyperbole: "We'll never know whether anybody was a good novelist or a bad novelist in this period because there's nobody left to do the necessary reading."[1]

During that winter of his discontent, Vidal's agent suggested he write for television, a medium with which he was totally unfamiliar. He promptly purchased a TV set, watched one play, and prepared a script for *Studio One.* On February 15, 1954, Gore Vidal became part of what is nostalgically called The Golden Age of Television, that brief period in the 1950's when live drama entered the home and every American was a first-nighter. The play was "Dark Possession," a melodrama about a schizophrenic female who wrote threatening letters to her malevolent half. "Dark Possession" was so popular it was repeated on other programs, including *Matinee Theatre;* it also won the approval of John Crosby, the dean of television critics, and soon Vidal joined the golden circle of Paddy Chayefsky, Horton Foote, Rod Serling, and Reginald Rose.

It was 1948 again, and Vidal was back in the columns. *The New York Times, Newsweek, TV Guide,* and *Variety* carried stories about the versatile novelist who switched from print to the twenty-one-inch screen with amazing ease. A few critics scoffed at the "Brooks Brothers Generation" who chose to sign up rather than sell out; but for the most part, the journalists welcomed the new breed of television writer—former novelists and would-be playwrights—who were elevating the taste of the nation. Vidal never assumed the role of the man of letters slumming on the tube. Although he boasted that he had earned more money in one year of writing TV dramas than he had in a decade of fiction, he never denied that the novel was his first love; it was, as he told a *Daily News* interviewer (June 23, 1957), "the most satisfactory and the purest form of art."

Despite his predilection for the novel, Vidal was also sincere when he rhapsodized on the virtues of live television, which turned the solitary writer on the Hudson into a social animal who had to confer with cast and crew. At times the rhapsodist became a prophet, and the columnists recorded his predictions as if they were Sibylline oracles. Since television would be the main source of drama until the millennium, he advised beginning writers to sign with the top agencies and encouraged his colleagues in fiction to explore the tube, if they could learn how to placate the sponsors and circumvent the controversial.

He even envisioned his own television show, *Monograph*, a half-hour program where the author would act as host-narrator, illustrating the nature of choreography with clips from Maria Tallchief in *The Nutcracker*, explaining the art of playwrighting, or discussing any topic that struck his fancy. Had *Monograph* materialized, it would have been Gore Vidal's answer to *Camera Three*.

Vidal was so convinced television would usurp the other media that he advocated a repertory playhouse on tape for all the live dramas that strutted their hour before the camera. Unfortunately, his dream was never realized. Anyone attempting to write a history of early television drama will be dependent on the published scripts that read like one-act plays, a memory that idealizes when it falters, newspaper reviews on microfilm, or the kinescopes, if one can gain access to those shadowy reminders of a lost immediacy. It is unsettling to realize that during the so-called Golden Age a live drama died as soon as it was born. Vidal thought tape would be the solution: "a play which is broadcast live will be accurately recorded and reshown."[2] The era of videotape has arrived, and with it very little worth retaining.

In 1956, Vidal made one of his saddest predictions: "In time, poets will write for television and if verse plays are possible in this century, they will find their audience through television. . . ."[3] Whoever said Gore Vidal was not an optimist?

It is difficult to determine exactly how many television plays Vidal authored between 1954 and 1960. Within a year of his debut, he admitted to twenty-five "signed" scripts and five or six under pseudonyms. In 1955 he published eight of them in a collection called *Visit to a Small Planet and Other Television Plays;* according to the preface, the number had reached "nearly thirty." The plays were both originals and adaptations, the latter netting him $2500 per script—a handsome compensation for bringing Stevenson, Hemingway, Faulkner, and Molnar to the masses.

As an adapter, Vidal had the popularizer's ability to reduce a work to its central theme without disturbing its complexity. When he was asked to adapt Faulkner's "Smoke" for *Suspense* (May 4, 1954), he cut through the dense prose to the core of the story—the rivalry between two brothers and their mutual hatred of their father. He treated Faulkner's "Barn Burning" in the same way, never subordinating the anguish of young Sarty Snopes to the amorality of his father. Between February and July 1955, he had adapted Henry James' *The Turn of the Screw*, Stephen Crane's "The Blue Hotel," the Kaufman-Ferber *Stage Door*, John P. Marquand's *Sincerely, Willis Wayde*, Hemingway's *A Farewell to Arms*, and Stevenson's *The Strange Case of Dr. Jekyll and Mr. Hyde*.

Vidal's favorite adaptation was *The Turn of the Screw*, which he did for *Omnibus*. He allowed the governess to tell her own story as she did in the novella, but he still had to answer the question critics have always posed about the ghosts: Whom did they haunt, the children or the governess? Vidal followed the hallucination theory: the ghosts existed for the governess alone. The spinsterish neuroticism Geraldine Page brought to the role underscored Edmund Wilson's thesis that the lady was transferring her sexual frustration to her wards.

The original scripts of 1955 reflected a world Vidal knew thoroughly—the South, where a faded heroine clings to a symbolic gazebo as if it were Chekhov's cherry orchard ("Summer Pavilion") and where corrupt politicians gain control of a state ("State of Confusion") or burn down an opponent's house ("A Sense of Justice"). His favorite original drama was "The Death of Billy the Kid," written for *Philco Television Playhouse*. It was an unsuccessful attempt to rework the saga of William Bonney into an anthropological passion play where the rival, Sheriff Pat Garrett, destroyed the Year King and replaced him as the popular hero. "The Death of Billy the Kid" had all the rhythms of tragic inevitability without the choreography of the tragic dance. Billy moves slowly, almost gracefully, toward a death that becomes painfully mythic when an omniscient drunk waxes biblical and compares the outlaw to Samson.

Aficionados of the Age of Chayefsky will always associate Vidal with "Visit to a Small Planet," which ranks with "Marty," Horton Foote's "A Young Lady of Property," and Rod Serling's "Patterns" as proof that television had its Camelot before it became the boob tube. Vidal had a great deal of difficulty getting the script past the sponsors, many of whom either found the satire too offensive or the subject matter too disquieting, no doubt recalling the doomsday atmosphere generated by "War of the Worlds" (1938). "They [the sponsors] have a horror of ideas, of anything smacking of originality, of innovation," Vidal railed in 1957 as he remembered an ad man who seriously believed television drama should be mediocre so it would not detract from the commercials.

Goodyear Television Playhouse finally produced "Visit to a Small Planet," which, despite its *deus ex machina* ending, still remains one of the finest examples of satire from the torpid Eisenhower days, when the main target of travesty was Marilyn Monroe. "Visit" was a darkly comic view of the flying saucer hysteria that was the meteoric counterpart of McCarthyism. Kreton, the visitor, planned to arrive in America on the eve of the Civil War; but by a chronological confusion attributable to the absence of clock time in outer space, he lands in Maryland in the mid-fifties. Kreton is the Margaret Mead of his unnamed planet; he regards the United States as a delightfully primitive society in the first stages of civilization. Telepathic and polylingual (he can even communicate with cats), Kreton calmly announces he has come to engineer a major war that will allow Americans to destroy each other and thus satisfy their need for violence: "I have returned to the dark ages of an insignificant planet simply because I want the glorious excitement of being among you and revelling in your savagery! There is murder in all your hearts and I love it!"⁴

Fortunately, the holocaust is prevented (or delayed) by the arrival of another visitor from space who carts Kreton back to eternity, explaining sheepishly that the retarded lad had escaped from his interplanetary nursery.

Contrary to what Vidal thought of the sponsors' lack of imagination, their uneasiness about "Visit to a Small Planet" suggested they knew the play was more than a science fiction comedy. The landing of a spacecraft in a Maryland rose garden was only the prelude to a comic parable of America's desire for self-destruction—a desire that was discreetly veiled by the spurious religiosity of the decade and the prayers for peace that were emanating from every corner of the globe. When Kreton observed that our "deepest pleasure is violence," he was stating in a more civilized way what H. Rap Brown expressed in his now classic simile: "Violence is as american as cherry pie."

Although Cyril Ritchard played Kreton with a Restoration foppery that made the character alien to the mid-twentieth century, one had the disquieting feeling the dandified visitor was the mythic embodiment of the American mind. Kreton was everything Americans aspire to be—drawing room wits, brilliant conversationalists, and more knowledgeable about their country than the goddamn foreigners. Unfortunately, he was also a mental retardate.

On February 7, 1957, Vidal's dramatization of his television comedy premiered in New York. *Visit to a*

Small Planet was his first Broadway play; it was also an immediate success. The hour-long script was expanded into a three-act comedy that incorporated every conceivable device to satisfy the sci-fi addict, the Manhattan sophisticate, and the out-of-towner. A vase rises in the air, a globe explodes, the romantic leads pack their suitcases with phone books and shack up in a motel, and satiric lines singe the stage without burning it up.

To protect an $80,000 investment, Vidal transformed his antiwar satire into a fun-house trip through the bellicose mind. Yet he did it in such a way that enlistees could laugh at Kreton's attempt to militarize a young pacifist by singing "Comin' in on a Wing and a Prayer" without ever realizing, at least while the play was in progress, that they had been seduced by similar propaganda.

No longer was America the tentacled monster of the world, but rather "people" in general. Thus the audience could laugh less nervously because the scapegoat was that universal bogy called Man. Kreton ceased being an American nightmare and became a global one. At the end of Act I, the visitor stated his position on *Homo sapiens,* not to any member of the Spelding family, but to Rosemary the cat—as good a symbol as any of creeping imperialism:

I simply dote on people. Why? Because of their primitive addiction to violence, because they seethe with emotions which I find bracing and intoxicating. For countless ages I have studied them and now I'm here to experience them firsthand, to wallow shamelessly in their steaming emotions . . . and to have fun, fun, fun!

In the television version, Kreton held a mirror up to America that reflected an image of its latent violence; but in the play, Kreton, a critic of the world at large, has come to promote nuclear war. America is not the only major power to stand before his tribunal; she is merely one of the "people."

Visit to a Small Planet was completely fashioned out of dream material. The play was a throwback to the sleep world where events multiply confusedly like the leaves of a beanstalk, familiar faces melt away and transmogrify, and actions wrench themselves loose from the fastenings of logic before the dreamer awakens sharply or wills himself into reality. Ellen Spelding, the ingenue, having learned some of Kreton's tricks of telepathy, makes contact with Delton 4, who arrives, like a Euripidean *deus ex machina*, to remove the visitor before he effects universal destruction. By an act of the will, Ellen steers the play, which had taken a detour into black comedy, back on the road to a blissful dénouement. Vidal, of course, has had the last laugh. By substituting telepathy for religious belief, Ellen performs an act of faith that saves the planet. No doubt her act also redeemed the play for loyal Americans and particularly for the Christophers, who were encouraging everyone to light one little candle and brighten up the world.

Nineteen fifty-seven was not only the year of Vidal's first Broadway success; it was also the year he completed his most ambitious television play. The script, originally written for *Playhouse 90*, was based on his grandfather's life; it had several working titles, including "The Story of Senator Gore," "The Indestructible Mr. Gore," "The Blind Senator," and "The Light in the Dark." Thomas Pryor Gore was an American legend, and Vidal presented him as such in a drama that combined the omniscient narrator of *Our Town* with the visionary pioneers, feckless heroines, and moustached villains of the movie Western.

At ten, "Guv," as young Tom Gore was called, was an accomplished declaimer of Shakespeare, a page in the Mississippi Senate, and a partially blind stoic ("Who needs two eyes anyway?"). He became completely sightless at eleven when he peered down the barrel of a toy gun that discharged a miniature spear. Yet he went off to Lebanon College in Tennessee, always finding a friend to read him Cicero, and by 1891 he was ready to practice law.

Gore chose to practice in Texas because it was heavily populist. When he was a child, his father made him swear on the bullet that wounded him at Shiloh that he would always be a son of populism. Before he was twenty-five, Gore ran for Congress on the populist ticket. He might have won if it had not been for a trumped-up charge of seduction. Although the charge was dismissed, the stigma remained, and Thomas Pryor Gore's political career in Texas was over.

He courted and married Nina Kay, who read to him, as his grandson would later do in Rock Creek Park, such engrossing works as a history of the English language. By 1901 the Gores—father, son, and bride—were in Oklahoma. With his father's aid, Gore set up a practice to help the settlers with their claims. When he announced he would run for the Senate as a Democrat, the inevitable break occurred between father and son. "There is a world elsewhere," Gore proclaimed, forever destroying the magic power of "the bullet that struck the people."

The Oklahoma campaign was no less turbulent than the Texas one. Gore was offered a bribe to support a land sale that would deprive the Indians of their property.

His opponents planned to revive the old seduction scandal, but discretion somehow prevailed. And at thirty-seven the blind Thomas Pryor Gore became Oklahoma's first United States Senator.

This dramatization of Senator Gore's life never materialized on *Playhouse 90*. The original script was too elaborate for television, although it would have made a spectacular film biography at a time when the genre was still popular. A shorter and much tighter version called "The Indestructible Mr. Gore" was televised on *Sunday Showcase* (December 13, 1959) with William Shatner in the title role and Vidal himself as narrator: "I'm Gore Vidal. And this is the town of Corsicana, Texas, in the year 1892."

The original chronicle became an hour-long memory play ending with a peroration of eloquent simplicity:

Gore's long life passed as swiftly in his own phrase as "the snowflakes upon the river." But he is still remembered and he is missed not only for himself but for what he was, as my grandmother who is watching this play tonight knows best of all.

The revised *Sunday Showcase* script in the archives of The State Historical Society of Wisconsin bears the scrawled signature of the Senator's wife and her imprimatur: "I have read the script herein and have no objections to being portrayed as Nina."

In the mid-fifties, Vidal, after making Paddy Chayefsky's ten-best list of the most important TV writers in the country, added the scenario to a repertory that was gradually encompassing every literary form. He signed a four-year contract with MGM in 1955, and the columnists began recording his *bons mots* about Hollywood:

"I'm very impressed with the movie people. They have not lived up to my expectations."[5] His first screenplay was *The Catered Affair* (1956), based on Chayefsky's well-known television drama. The film was a triumph for Debbie Reynolds, but little was said of Vidal's script which, in Bosley Crowther's opinion, "only puts a few more whorls on the design of the Chayefsky TV play."

Vidal divides his scenarios into two categories: "Those that *are* all mine and those that *were* all mine." The former include his accurate but generally ignored treatment of the Dreyfus case, *I Accuse* (1958), which premiered in New York on the Loew's circuit as part of a double bill with *The Safecracker*; *Suddenly Last Summer* (1959), falsely attributed to the combined efforts of Vidal and Tennessee Williams ("It was based on Tennessee's play, and his name was good for box office"); the screen version of *The Best Man* (1964); and *Last of the Mobile Hot-Shots* (1970), which clarified somewhat the biblical obscurantism of Williams' *The Seven Descents of Myrtle*.

It is commonly thought that Vidal turned his television play "The Death of Billy the Kid" into a film, *The Left Handed Gun* (1958); but the credits attribute the script to Leslie Stevens "from a television play by Gore Vidal." He adapted Daphne Du Maurier's *The Scapegoat* (1959), with director Robert Hamer receiving credit for the screenplay. Vidal also contributed a third of the dialogue to *Ben Hur* (1959) and spent three months in Paris working on René Clément's disaster *Is Paris Burning?* (1966) which emerged as a trilingual monstrosity with five scenarists sharing the responsibility for one of the most unintelligible films ever produced.

Suddenly Last Summer was Vidal's favorite scenario; the extremely well-crafted script proved he knew film was the adult version of "Show and Tell." Williams' one-act fable of cannibalism and perversion was superb theatre but totally unfilmable in its original form. The single set reduced motivation to exposition and created certain incongruities, such as a doctor's first encounter with his patient in the garden of a New Orleans mansion rather than in a hospital. While a garden is the perfect setting for the dénouement, it is hardly suitable for a medical consultation.

Williams' play had three main characters—Dr. Cukrowicz, a specialist in prefrontal lobotomy; Violet Venable, a millionairess who promised to finance his research provided he lobotomize her babbling niece; and Catharine Holly, the niece who was committed to a mental institution because of the fantastic story she told about the death of her aunt's dilettante son, Sebastian.

Vidal had to rethink the play in terms of cinema. Williams' Dr. Cukrowicz was a cipher—noble but nebulous. His only function was to feed cues to Mrs. Venable and Catharine. To dramatize a sense of commitment that Williams only implied, Vidal did not begin with the doctor's visit to Mrs. Venable as the playwright did, but with an operating sequence where Cukrowicz (Montgomery Clift) was seen performing a lobotomy under deplorably primitive conditions. A dedicated surgeon should have an appropriate foil, and Vidal invented the character of Dr. Lawrence J. Hockstader (Albert Dekker), the sweaty superintendent of Lion's View Hospital, who was willing to sacrifice Catharine's sanity for Mrs. Venable's million-dollar foundation.

Early in the play, Williams had Catharine speak vacantly about Sebastian's penchant for blondes: "Fed up with dark ones, famished for light ones: that's how he

talked about people, as if they were—items on a menu."
Exposition was clearly the reason for her reverie; it was
hardly the kind of small talk one would make with a
grim-faced nun standing nearby. Vidal knew it was the
sort of rambling disclosure someone would blurt out
under sedation; accordingly, in the film, Catharine
(Elizabeth Taylor) begins her reminiscence in the hospital after Cukrowicz has given her an injection.

Williams entrusted the curtain line to Dr. Cukrowicz:
"I think we ought at least to consider the possibility that
the girl's story could be true." In the film, it is spoken by
Dr. Hockstader, the converted skeptic. Obviously, Cukrowicz knew she was telling the truth; furthermore, he
has fallen in love with her. And so the film ends with an
exquisite long shot of Catharine and Dr. Cukrowicz fac-
ing each other in Sebastian's tropical garden that now
seems almost Edenic.

Katharine Hepburn, who played Mrs. Venable,
should be eternally grateful to Vidal for giving her the
most Olympian entrance on celluloid. Like the goddess
from the machine, she descends in an elevator, her Bryn
Mawr voice floating down the shaft:

Well, it seems that the Emperor of Byzantium when he received people in audience had a throne which, during the
conversation, would mysteriously rise in the air, to the con-
sternation of the visitors. But, as we are living in a democracy,
I reverse the procedure; I don't rise. I come down.

⟨ 7

Christ and Anti-Christ

REGINA DURHAM'S prediction of a new messiah in *The Judgment of Paris* anticipated the religious revival of the 1950's, a decade that began with the Holy Year, as christened by Pope Pius XII, and the Korean police action misnamed by President Truman. During an era when Fulton Sheen was as popular as Arthur Godfrey, no one ever believed another religion could replace Christianity. It could only occur in myth or in the fifties equivalent—the science fiction film.

The displacement of Christianity by a dark humanism intrigued Vidal enough to make him contemplate the perverse joke history could play on a culture whose collapse, as T. S. Eliot warned, would plunge the world into "many centuries of barbarism." As a kinsman of Petronius and Apuleius, Vidal would find a delectable irony in the growth of a new religion that began in much the same way as Christianity did—with a relative unknown whose initials were, appropriately enough, J. C.

In *Messiah* (1954), Vidal was sounding the foundations of the devout fifties, when television embraced faith healers and Mickey Mousers alike. Was it possible that America clapped hands and welcomed Jesus from fear instead of love? The U.F.O.'s that circled the land were no less terrifying than the prodigies Livy recorded in his *History of Rome;* and omens have a way of bringing even agnostics to their knees. The science fiction films of the period mirrored America's fear of annihilation—the voice of God interrupting a radio broadcast to demand a return to the old mores *(The Next Voice You Hear,* 1950); a visitor from another planet landing in Washington with an ultimatum to ban the bomb *(The Day the Earth Stood Still,* 1951); the sudden wave of spirituality that inundated the country when America discovered God ruled Mars *(Red Planet Mars,* 1952); monsters dislodged from their habitats by atomic tests *(The Beast from 20,000 Fathoms,* 1953); a Martian invasion of California, where the only survivors were those who sought refuge in a Catholic church *(The War of the Worlds,* 1953). Peace, that uneasy period between wars, would last only if men cultivated the virtues of yore. A totemic Jehovah demanded white bucks and crewcuts; for the recalcitrant he had a soundstage full of mutants—giant ants, vegetable men, oversized mollusks and, of course, Godzilla, that child of the Orient we welcomed to our breasts as atonement for Hiroshima.

While the horror films of the forties were sadistic, those of the fifties were bogusly religious. The operations the mad doctors at Universal were performing in their eerie sanatariums between 1941 and 1945 symbolized the experiments the *Uebermenschen* were conducting at Dachau and Auschwitz. The horror films of the fifties also reflected their age. Embedded in these movies was the terror of death; and the ending where the fearful acknowledged the existence of a Higher Power had a peculiarly biblical quality about it. If the horror film is the metaphor of the age as well as a reflection of its unconscious desires, it is clear from such movies that what Americans in the fifties yearned for was a messiah —someone who could either make life bearable in a nuclear world or make death palatable to a nuclear people. *Messiah* translated this unconscious wish into an actuality; if the science fiction films of the fifties had any ulterior message, it was that Christianity had failed to assuage man's fear of extinction and that its main function seemed to be that of a *deus ex machina* or an eleventh-hour reprieve—but only for the chosen.

Messiah begins around the year 2000 A.D. Eugene Luther is living in Luxor under the name of Richard Hudson. He is racing against time to complete his account of the new religion that swept across Europe and America during the 1950's. Age and infirmity militate against an exhaustive chronicle, but perhaps he can offer the world "a relative truth," if not an absolute one.

The memoirist recalls a summer afternoon in the early fifties when he was Eugene Luther, a resident of the Hudson River Valley, sometime student of history, and luncheon companion of the ageless Clarissa Lessing. Luther's world admits of no vista but the historical, and Clarissa's of none but the mythic. He is a leftover from the age of reason who cannot adapt to the mysticism of the new decade. Clarissa, the adroit matchmaker, introduces him to Iris Mortimer, whose name evokes a rainbow goddess as well as a funeral director. It is Iris who tells Luther about a mesmeric ex-embalmer in California called John Cave.

Since *Messiah* is a journal within a novel or a series of recollections within a memoir, one might expect a certain disharmony between the novelist's voice and the memoirist's. Yet they synchronize perfectly, and what Vidal has achieved in *Messiah* is quite unusual in futuristic fiction. Eugene Luther's voice in mid-century matches Richard Hudson's in 2000 A.D., and both emanate from the well-modulated persona of Eugene Luther Gore Vidal. The memoirist's voice can detach itself from its chronicle, questioning its aesthetic and querying its ability to describe accurately. When the memory grows dim, the voice checks itself and tries to disentangle the reality from the illusion. The speaker scrutinizes his portrait of Iris, wondering whether he is "really getting her right." In the early fifties, she was neither the rainbow goddess of myth nor the angel of death; she was merely an ex-fashion editor lunching with Clarissa and himself: "The truth is that we met; we became friends; we lunched amiably and the future cast not one shadow across the mahogany table around which we sat . . ."[1]

The three of them became evangelists for John Cave, the American primitive, whose message was simply that death is good. But Cave, like any American product, needed merchandising. In the fifties, this meant the hard sell and a half-hour spot on television, where the messiah could mesmerize with a voice that radio and film had perfected into an instrument of seduction. And so it was that Cavite, Inc., was born, with its directors, shareholders, Residents, Communicators and, of course, its own

bible—The Testament of Cavesword. The power behind
the throne was the apostolic Paul Himmell, a former
Hollywood publicist, who was zealously aided by Luther, Clarissa, Iris, and the Jungian Dr. Stockharin.

Suicides increase throughout the country as America
discovers Cavesway, the beatific end-it-all the faithful
can practice in a special Center. Given the popularity of
Cavesway, it would seem logical for the founder of the
movement to practice what he had been preaching and
make the ritual leap from scapegoat to God. When Himmell orders Cave to swallow the death pill Dr. Stockharin has invented, he refuses and hurls the container at
the Jungian, who is a true believer in the archetypal triad
and therefore fires three shots at the messiah.

Cave is cremated, and his ashes scattered across the
United States. A council meets to determine the future
of Cavesword: will it emphasize life or death? A tie results, and Iris, like Athena in the *Eumenides*, breaks it by
voting for the latter. Thanatos triumphs, the churches
come tumbling down, and Regina Durham's prophecy is
fulfilled.

Luther's memoir was intentionally anti-Christian; it
was designed to convey "a relative truth as opposed to
that monstrous testament the one-half world believes"
(p. 2). Yet Luther himself edited a similarly "monstrous"
Testament that became the Bible of Cavesword, the
translation of the founder's inarticulate ramblings into
finished prose. It is in this respect that *Messiah* achieves
an ambivalence lacking in most futuristic fiction that
veers off into satire, phantasmagoria, or simple-minded
fantasy. Far from being a modern heretic, Luther was
closer to St. Luke, the most literary of the evangelists,
who gave the words of Jesus a grace and a rhetorical

polish they obviously could never have had in their spoken form.

John Cave, like Jesus Christ, required evangelists to codify his ideas; yet neither messiah had any control over the Testament his evangelists published. A theogony is basically God reconsidered by man; and more often than not, God poeticized by man. Consider the New Testament, which has been subjected to as much misinterpretation as *Hamlet*. If Paul Himmell the ex-publicist is modeled after St. Paul the ex-Pharisee, then Vidal is comparing Himmell's perversion of Cavesword with Paul's Hellenization of Christ's teachings.

Vidal is hardly an admirer of Pauline Christianity, which "tried to put the lid on sex," as he phrased it in his essay "The Twelve Caesars" (1959).[2] Yet St. Paul was no more responsible for Christianity's growth from a sect to a corporation than Paul Himmell was for Cavesword's growth from a middle-class panacea to an ideology. Once its doctrines are to be bound between the covers of a Testament, a religion has no other choice than to systematize them. Vidal is suggesting that the creation of the New Testament irrevocably changed a mystery religion into a body corporate—a charge echoed by many modern theologians who believe that if Jesus Christ could ever return to the twentieth century, he would be utterly baffled by the edifice his successors built on the Rock called Peter.

While it is dreadfully platitudinous to say an author was "ahead of his time," Vidal clearly was. His belief that organized religion has failed the individual by becoming bureaucratic is hardly anathema to enlightened churchmen like Harvey Cox, Karl Rahner, and Hans Küng. While the Death of God theology did not extinguish all the candles in the churches, it at least offered a less sepulchral light. Eucharistic banquets on kitchen tables, folk masses, and encounter sessions in church auditoriums are alternatives to the services where the celebrant literally turned his back on the congregation and mumbled in badly pronounced Latin.

Messiah is actually more critical of ecclesiastical hierarchy than it is of Christianity, which, in its inception at least, was as salutary as Cavesword. Yet one question remains: If Cavesword is Christianity's replacement, what did it accomplish that its predecessor did not? It would have been more in keeping with the cycle of the eternal return for a new paganism to arise in mid-century and overwhelm the See of Peter with "the glory that was Greece and the grandeur that was Rome." As it happened, Cavesword was nothing but Christianity pushed to its logical conclusion. Primitive Christianity was based on synthesis and transformation—the conversion of classical philosophy to the service of God and the metamorphosis of the pagan gods in church-sponsored art. Cavesword was founded on the same principle of synthesis—the reconciliation of classical humanism with the teachings of Jesus Christ. In this respect, it scarcely differed from the attempts of the Church Fathers to press pagan man against the bosom of Mother Church.

The very name "Cavesword" suggests a synthesis of classical antiquity and Christianity. "Cave" harks back to the subterranean region of Plato's *Republic,* where the ignorant sit in chains and see only dim reflections of reality. "Word" evokes the beginning of the Gospel According to St. John: "In the beginning was the Word, and the Word was with God; and the Word was God." This is the cardinal doctrine of Christianity—God becoming Man through the Incarnation. Cavesword grew out of a pastiche of Platonism and Christianity, both of which favored spirit over flesh and the perfect world over the one we know. A knowledge of the Word releases the prisoners in the cave and elevates them to a better understanding of the Logos, regarded as either human reason or a divine plan.

Cavesword was also an attempt to apply Plato's theories in the *Republic* to the modern world. The new religion advocated controlled breeding and the abolition of the family, two of the main features of Plato's utopia. Just as Plato's ideal state had its Guardians and Auxiliaries, Cavesword had its Residents and Communicators. From Seneca, Cavesword adopted the Stoic philosophy of suicide as a rational departure from life. Obviously, the average slob could no more choose Cavesway than the unphilosophical Roman could elect the Stoic suicide. It was reserved for the true Cavites, who could check in at a Center and obtain a lethal but painless drug that allowed a full hour of conversation before it took effect. It would be a less decadent version of Seneca's own method—"that ineluctable warm bath with open veins," as Vidal once termed it.[3]

Like any eclectic system, Cavesword was doomed to a series of rifts, schisms, and synods. Once Luther broke with Iris on the doctrine of Cavesway, he became a "lutherist." His name was expunged from the Testament which was largely his creation. Soon lutherists were synonymous with heretics; they were lobotomized by the Squad of Belief in much the same way as heretics were burned by the Inquisition—lobotomy being more civilized than the auto-da-fé.

Not only did the Cavites falsify history; they also

mythologized it. Before Cave became the American messiah, he nearly killed a man in a hit-and-run accident in California. His brief imprisonment later became known as the Time of Persecution, and the conversations he had with Iris Mortimer in his cell were idealized as the "Prison Dialogues."

Reflections behind bars are always penned in guiltless blood. The reasons for incarceration soon become historically unimportant as time embosses them with an antique sheen. The fact that we speak of Plato's "Prison Dialogues" or of certain of St. Paul's letters as the "Prison Epistles" indicates that we are all mythopoetic at heart. John Cave was fortunate in having disciples who canonized him by translating his imprisonment into a Time of Persecution, an ideal title for a chapter heading in a catechism.

Religions become polarized when the Great Mother vies with the Sky God as the object of worship. Early Greek mythology, with its cosmic struggle between the primal female and the usurping patriarch, was no less bipolar than Christianity, with its cult of Mary and its worship of Jesus. On the one hand, there was the old Jesuit motto, "To Jesus through Mary," for those who found the mother more accessible than her son; on the other, there was Mariolatry, for those who found the mother more divine than her son. Recently, Mary has been, as the hip theologians say, put in her place; she is acknowledged as the mother of the messiah but not as the coordinator of his mission.

The cult of the White Goddess always attracts mental castrates, a good number of whom converted to Cavesword. Consequently, the Cavites split into two factions: those who worshiped the mother (Iris Mortimer) and those who venerated the son (John Cave). Again Vidal has shown how history becomes myth with the passage of time; because of the human need to invent a union where none exists, a tradition arose within half a century that Iris and Cave were mother and son.

Messiah is a novel only the unemancipated could call anti-Christian. Vidal has always posed as a foe of religion, although once on a talk show he rather sincerely advocated that paintings of the resurrection replace those of the crucifixion in Catholic homes because rebirth is a more sublime concept than death. Yet in his superb demolition piece, "Two Immoralists: Orville Prescott and Ayn Rand" (1961), he wrote: ". . . I doubt if even the most anti-Christian freethinker would want to deny the ethical value of Christ in the Gospels. To reject that Christ is to embark on dangerous waters indeed."[4]

By establishing parallels between the lives of Jesus Christ and John Cave (a three-year ministry, evangelists, a following that swelled into a congregation, the scapegoat death of the founder, a historical foundation that subsequently became mythical), Vidal has traced the evolution of a religion from a secret society to a corporate structure. Cave's position, " 'Our quarrel is not with Christ but with his keepers,' " was no different from that of the Catonsville Nine. Vidal, the Petronian pagan, was more of a Christian than he thought; actually, he knew more about Christianity than most churchgoers did in the early 1950's.

At the end of *Messiah*, Luther's memoir is almost complete. The reconstruction of the past or "the relative truth" has brought the memoirist to an absolute truth of his own. As the main author of the Testament, Luther realizes he was responsible for the image of John Cave

for those who had never known him. It was Eugene
Luther, not John Cave, who really was the messiah; Cave
was a literary construct, the creation of an evangelist.
One is left wondering whether Matthew, Mark, Luke,
and John ever experienced a similar epiphany, for they
created the Christ the world has come to know.

Before Eugene Luther became a proselyte to Cavesword, he had been contemplating a biography of Julian
the Apostate, who attempted a noble but abortive revival
of Hellenism during his brief reign as Emperor of Rome
(361–63 A.D.). Like Philip Warren in *The Judgment of Paris*,
who abandoned his comic novel about the Lady of the
Blue Notes, Luther abandoned Julian; and like Warren,
who discovered the incongruities of comedy in real-life
adventures, Luther found the equivalent of Julian's mystical paganism in Cavesword. Similarly, Vidal, "the least
autobiographical of novelists," converted his 1948 *Wanderjahr* into a picaresque novel, and his early research on
the Apostate into a dark fable. With the publication of
Julian (1964), no one could doubt that Eugene Luther
Gore Vidal finished what Eugene Luther began.

While Luther was searching the skies for flying sau-
cers and fretting about the decline of the West, Vidal was
also meditating on the portents from heaven and the
neo-paganism they heralded. It seemed that in the early
fifties America was marching on to decadence; Vidal,
always one to accede to "what the age demanded,"
turned to the ultimate in decadence—the literature of
the Roman Empire. It was almost as if he were attempting to find a parallel between Rome's deterioration and
America's. The Empire had a rhetorical tradition that at
least provided the consolation of literacy when the shadows began to fall, while America never knew the joys of

the trivium except in the debased form of political oratory. It is quite possible we will never experience a decadence simply because we do not know enough about the refinement of style to appreciate its overrefinement.

The appeal of Petronius, Apuleius, and the other writers of the Empire lay in their insistence on some literary standards, despite the direction the Latin of their day was taking. Even archaisms and exotic coinages were better than spastic grunts. In matters of language, Vidal has always been a purist, castigating Faulkner for using "euphemistic" for "euphonious" in *Requiem for a Nun* and taking Arthur Miller to task for the faulty grammar in his "Introduction to the *Collected Plays.*" At the Fourth Literary Symposium that *Esquire* sponsored at the University of Michigan, Vidal inveighed against the mindless prose of some of his contemporaries:

But we are nothing if not permissive. We've all had to get used to what I call demotic writing, where any word is as good as any other word, and garrulity, since it is so common in life, must then be virtuous in literature.[5]

Naturally Vidal would be attracted to the fourth century, when the pagan rhetoricians battled the Christian apologists for reasons that had as much to do with the preservation of the ancient style as they did with the preservation of the ancient religion. To Vidal, the period was crucial for anyone with a Christian upbringing and an allegiance to the classical past, as he explained in the "Author's Note" to *Julian:* "During the fifty years between the accession of Julian's uncle Constantine the Great and Julian's death at thirty-two, Christianity was established. For better or worse, we are today very much the result of what they were then."[6]

The triumph of Christianity was never as simple as Cecil B. De Mille's depiction of it in *The Sign of the Cross* (1932). While the martyrologies extol the generals who embraced Christianity at the expense of their lives, there were enough adherents to the old regime to thwart its progress. In the third century, Elagabalus tried to organize a solar religion, and Aurelian promoted a Cult of the Unconquered Sun, designating December 25 as its birthday. But the most vigorous opponent of Christianity, or rather of its claim to be a universal religion, was Julian, whom the Fathers called the Apostate because of his fanatical devotion to paganism.

Julian fascinated Vidal in a way no other historical figure could. Perhaps he found a kinsman in an Emperor who at six knew his religion with a catechetical accuracy and at thirty was sacrificing cattle to pagan deities. But as Eugene Luther was forced to admit, the source material for Julian's life was overwhelming. In addition to Julian's own writings, there was Ammianus Marcellinus' chronicle of his reign in the *Res Gestae;* Libanius' flattering orations on the young man who emulated his style; Gregory Nazianzen's invective; and Cyril of Alexandria's polemic, to cite only a few. There was also the uncritical stand of the pre-Vatican II Catholic schools: "Constantine, *Si;* Julian, *No.*"

For nine years the source material also baffled Vidal. Instead of fictionalizing the Apostate's life, he wrote *Messiah.* But during that highly prolific period when he was turning out television scripts and scenarios and revising *Visit to a Small Planet* for Broadway, he was preparing for the novel he would eventually write by reading the Greek authors Julian would have known and familiarizing himself with the history of the fourth century. In 1959 he began his *magnum opus,* and five years later it was published—his first best seller since *The City and the Pillar.*

Structurally, *Julian* is not only Vidal's most complex work; it is one of the most elaborate historical novels ever conceived. In Robert Graves' *I, Claudius* (1934) and Thornton Wilder's *The Ides of March* (1948), the novel of classical antiquity found its twin models. While *I, Claudius* was a fictional autobiography of the emperor, *The Ides of March* was an epistolary novel where the action was unfolded through a series of letters, journals, and even graffiti. The techniques Graves and Wilder used were not arbitrary; the ideal novel of antiquity should be written the way the ancients would have approached historical fiction—as a memoir or as a fluid progression of epistles, testimonies, and journal-entries similar to the primary sources a classical writer might come across in the imperial archives. The canon had been so well established that when John Hersey decided to fictionalize the bizarre plot to assassinate Nero in 65 A.D., he wrote *The Conspiracy* (1972) as a transcript of dispatches, intercepted letters, files, and interrogations.

As a novelist, Vidal was hardly impervious to influences; but in *Julian* he outstripped Graves and Wilder by combining their methods. *Julian* is neither a memoir nor an epistolary latticework, but something of both. Vidal offers three alternatives to the distorted portrait of the Emperor: Julian's memoir, Priscus' commentary on it, and Libanius' observations on both the memoir and the commentary. The structure of *Julian* is a microcosm of the controversy that has always raged about the Apostate; it is also Vidal's answer to the questions that have always plagued historians and writers of historical fiction: Whom should one believe, the subject or his commentators? The primary or the secondary sources? The teller, the tale, or the scholar?

Julian is like a triptych, with the memoir as the central panel flanked on one side by Priscus' commentary that emends and challenges the Apostate's version, and on the other by Libanius' recollections that complement and at times contradict both accounts. The effect is comparable to watching three newscasts transmitted simultaneously and from different points of view on a tripartite screen.

The novel begins in 380 A.D., seventeen years after Julian's death. The news of Emperor Theodosius' edict branding anyone a heretic who would not follow the Nicene Creed has just reached Libanius, the sophist of Antioch and Julian's best panegyrist. Although Libanius was too committed to Hellenism to embrace a religion that appealed mainly to the lower social strata, he had known Basil the Great and had taught John Chrysostom, both of whom were later canonized and numbered among the Doctors of the Church.

But the age of gifted pupils, even gifted Christians, had passed; and Latin, a barbaric tongue Libanius refused to learn, was replacing Greek in the academies. One last stand must be made against Christianity before it engulfed the world. "What happens to us personally is not important, but what happens to civilization is a matter of desperate concern" (p. 5), he wrote to Priscus who possessed the fragmentary memoir Julian had composed during the last four months of his life. The time had come for a vindication of Julian which they could accomplish by publishing the memoir along with a biography of the late Emperor.

Priscus, still potent at seventy-five and unwilling to

jeopardize his remaining years of virility, agreed to have the memoir copied for a fee but refused to involve himself in the publication: "I have no wish to be burned alive or stoned or tacked up to the door of a Christian church, or 'charnel house' as Julian used to call them" (p. 8). But because of his close association with Julian, whom he accompanied on the fatal Persian campaign of 363, he could not refrain from adding a commentary of his own.

Historically, there was no memoir, and if Julian ever composed any *Commentaries* on his Gallic campaigns, they have not survived. But Vidal's hypothetical text would certainly have won the Emperor's approval. Julian's memoir would probably have been a strange amalgam of historical commentary and spiritual autobiography, a hybrid of two of the most dissimilar works in Greek literature—Xenophon's *Anabasis* and Marcus Aurelius' *To Himself.* Vidal assumed such a memoir would have been as eclectic as Julian.

Marcus Aurelius began *To Himself* with a page of acknowledgments in which he thanked his grandfather, father, mother, and teachers for all they had given him. Julian, who admired *To Himself,* could easily have begun in the same vein:

From the example of my uncle the Emperor Constantine, called the Great, who died when I was six years old, I learned that it is dangerous to side with any party of the Galileans. ... From my mother Basilina I inherited my love of learning. ... From my cousin and predecessor, the Emperor Constantius, I learned to dissemble and disguise my true thoughts. (pp. 15–16)

While Marcus Aurelius only thanked those who trained him in virtue, Julian even acknowledged his teachers of vice. He quickly learned the art of dissembling from an event that transformed a six-year-old innocent into a political animal—his father's murder at the order of Emperor Constantius II.

Although the young Julian found a protector in Eusebius, bishop of Nicomedia, he and his half-brother Gallus still lived with the fear that someday they would share their father's fate. (Gallus did meet a bloody end, but he was such an inveterate sadist that it seemed only fitting he should be decapitated like a common thief.) Julian was more perturbed by the immorality of his father's murder than the crime itself. Constantius was Julian's cousin and a Christian Emperor; the discrepancy between "Thou Shalt Not Kill" and the flexible interpretation it was receiving in the imperial household compelled the child to see the dichotomy between Christian theory and practice. And when Julian witnessed a group of monks flogging two old men because they were heretics, he knew the message of Christ had been lost on the clergy.

During the fourth century, the Church was too busy quibbling about the Trinity to pay much attention to the Gospels. When George, bishop of Cappadocia, took over Julian's religious education, he drilled him in the Arian belief that Jesus was not of the same substance as the Father *(homoousios)* but merely of a similar substance *(homoiousios)*. Julian was taught to respect Arius and scoff at Athanasius, who devoted his life to promoting the consubstantiality of Father and Son. Ironically, Arius is now considered a heretic; and Athanasius, a saint and Doctor of the Church.

Vidal has isolated the beginnings of Julian's apostasy in his early exposure to Arianism, which he simply pushed to its logical conclusion: if Jesus is not of the same substance as the Father, then he obviously cannot be God. His negative view of Jesus was compounded by the endless arguments about his relationship to the Father—arguments that were as ludicrous as the speculations of the Schoolmen about the number of angels that could dance on the head of a pin. Julian's is the classic case of defection from the Church; his aversion to Christianity can be traced to a religious education that robbed God of his mystery and reduced his existence to question-and-answer form.

Julian wanted a God as warm and life-giving as the sun. His Christian tutor Mardonius cautioned him against Mithraism, "the most devilish of all the cults," with its anti-Trinity of the intelligible world, the sensible world, and the sun mediating between them; but Julian found the cult aesthetically superior to Christianity. When he was finally initiated into the Mysteries of Mithras at Ephesus, Julian had found his One God.

As a son of Homer, Julian could not forsake Hellenism for Mithraism. The Greeks had their Helios; the Persians, Mithras. So he combined them into one supreme being, Helios-Mithras. But Julian was also interested in the transcendent God whom Plotinus called The One. In short, he was attracted to any God who had no connection with Jesus Christ, and in his calmer moments he even spoke favorably of Yahweh. From this strange synthesis of Helios-Mithras and The One came a trinity that was even more abstruse than the triune God of the Christians: The One presiding over the intelligible world, Helios-Mithras occupying the center of the intermediary world, and the physical sun (the visible counterpart of Helios) governing the sensible world. The Church could always fall back on a three-leaf clover whenever it needed an analogy for the Trinity; but there was nothing in nature to help the neophyte understand the Julian triad. Furthermore, it is impossible to believe the new trinity would have been any improvement over Father, Son, and Holy Ghost; through a wild syncretism, Julian merely substituted one mystery for another.

Vidal explains Julian's eclecticism in terms of his education. By the time he was twenty, the age when he ceased being a Christian, Julian had been exposed to the most diversified faculty imaginable—Eusebius, who taught him the articles of a faith he would later reject; the Arian Bishop George, who encouraged his interest in the Neoplatonists by lending him manuscripts from his personal library; the eunuch Mardonius, who tutored him in the Greek classics; the charlatan Maximus, who initiated him into Mithraism; and of course, the sophist Libanius, whose rhetorical style he admired. Christianity, Hellenism, Neoplatonism, Mithraism, Sophistry: he tasted them all and remembered the distinctive flavor of each.

As Julian pursued his exotic syncretism, he became conscious of his own immortality and gravitated to any cult that would ensure it. He was initiated into the Eleusinian Mysteries, with their ritual baptisms, passion plays, and vision of a future life. Gradually the student of the mystery religions became a celebrant of the ancient rites, sacrificing animals even in time of famine and trying vainly to save the oracle of Delphi from the disrepute into which it had deservedly fallen.

In many respects, Julian reminds one of T. S. Eliot, the devout Anglo-Catholic defending the classical foundation of Western culture from the illiterates threatening to undermine it. Yet Eliot realized that Christian writers could not ignore the contributions of anthropology; in *The Waste Land*, he tried to unite Jesus Christ with the vegetation deities of myth. What he produced was a never-ending equation where Adonis = Osiris = Hyacinthus = The Fisher King = The Hanged Man of the Tarot pack = (ultimately) Jesus Christ, as if all of Frazer's hanged gods were identical and as if Jesus Christ were a Year Daimon born in winter and dismembered in spring. Just as Eliot attempted to stamp a sacramental character on the myth of Teiresias by working it into the Grail legend, Julian attempted to integrate the Olympians with the worship of Helios-Mithras. Zeus, the Sky God, became a creative force subservient to Helios and having no existence of his own; Athena, Dionysus, and Aphrodite became emanations from the One God.

In his "Seventh Oration," Julian compared myths to teething rings for children or water for parched land. Vidal's Julian expounds a similar belief: " 'After all, as educated men, we should realize that myths always stand for other things. They are toys for children teething' " (p. 338). Julian, like Eliot, never stopped teething. Both allegorized the myths, translating them into literary artifacts. But when a god becomes a poetic device, he is no longer a deity but an imaginative construct whose credibility is only as great as that of the work in which he functions. In the case of *The Waste Land*, only a student of comparative religion or the occult could accept Jesus as the Hanged Man of the Tarot. Certainly a simple believer could not, any more than an unlettered Greek of the fourth century could understand Julian's Aphrodite as the spirit of love and unity.

Julian's attempt to revive paganism was unsuccessful;

yet one must ask whether, if it had succeeded, his religion would have been any better than Christianity. Julian would be shocked to realize it, but he inherited all the excesses he deplored in Christianity. He prayed to Athena in time of need with the same fervor Catholics exhibit when they invoke St. Jude as the Patron of Hopeless Cases. While Jesus and the Virgin appeared to the saints, The Spirit of the Roman People appeared to Julian. There was little difference between Julian's appeasing the gods with sacrifices and a Catholic's requesting masses and votive lights for special intentions.

Julian aped the asceticism of the Desert Fathers by his abstemious diet and his preference for coarse blankets. After the death of his wife Helena, he became a celibate, dedicating his chastity to Cybele like a priest spurning the joys of marriage to serve God. He cultivated and practiced every quality of a Christian saint. Even Priscus knew what Julian had become: "Julian was Christian in everything except his tolerance of others. He was what the Christians would call a saint" (p. 89). In the end, he was Christianity's victim as well as its scourge.

The reader who thought *Julian* would be an anti-Christian tract on the order of Anatole France's *The Governor of Judea* was no doubt amazed by the sanity of the author's presentation. Vidal was too devoted a student of history to falsify it. Despite his sympathy for the Emperor, he was not blind to his defects. By using Priscus' commentary and Libanius' reminiscences to counterbalance the weight of the memoir, Vidal has provided as accurate a picture of the Apostate as one is likely to find.

Like mirrors reflecting the same image from different angles, Libanius and Priscus complement and emend, correct and amplify the Emperor's memoir. During the first year of the Gallic campaigns, Julian noticed he was developing a lust for battle, but Priscus has no recollection of his ever admitting a penchant for war. Julian seriously believed his reign would be an improvement upon his cousin's, but there were those, as Priscus observes, who preferred Constantius. Julian's edict forbidding Christians to teach the Classics found favor with Libanius but appalled Priscus: "Julian was quite right when he said that I opposed the Edict on Education. I thought it cruel, as well as impossible to regulate" (p. 362). Priscus soon began to wonder whether Julian's paganism would be any different from Christianity: "I suspect that had Julian lived, matters would have been just as they were under Constantius, only instead of being bored by quarrels about the nature of the trinity we would have had to listen to disputes about the nature of Zeus's sex life . . ." (p. 381).

Even Libanius, whose eulogies of Julian were at times downright fulsome, was revolted when the Emperor sacrificed oxen to Cybele in a ceremony that involved the flogging of a hundred youths. One is almost forced to agree with Gibbon's assessment in *The Decline and Fall of the Roman Empire:*

It is impossible to determine how far the zeal of Julian would have prevailed over his good sense and humanity; but, if we seriously reflect on the strength and spirit of the church, we shall be convinced that, before the emperor could have extinguished the religion of Christ, he must have involved his country in the horrors of a civil war.

Although Vidal has emphasized the theological confusion of the age as the key to Julian's apostasy, he did not ignore the Emperor's politics. *Julian* should be read in conjunction with "Barry Goldwater: A Chat" (1961), which contains Vidal's cameo sketch of the typical politician:

He is not at all like other men, though he must acquire as protective coloration the manners of his society; join in its rituals (Caesar, the atheist, was a solemn high priest and our own Calvin Coolidge wore an Indian war bonnet), exploit its prejudices and anticipate its hungers. . . . Finally, the politician must have that instinctive sense of occasion which is also the actor's art. To the right challenge he must have the right response.[7]

At six, Julian knew that if one were powerful enough, he could write his own exceptions to the Ten Commandments as Constantius did. Always fearing his devout cousin would terminate his life, Julian learned his catechism faithfully and impressed Bishop George as suitable material for the priesthood—an ideal haven in time of danger as the men who became divinity students during World War II and Korea can verify. Julian learned the art of deception without a handbook and cultivated "the actor's art" to survive. After Constantius adopted him as Caesar, Julian soon began to lie. During the pacification of Gaul, he invented battle instructions when none existed and pillaged towns to provide food for his mutinous troops. When his men wanted to proclaim him Augustus, he declined the honor; when they insisted, he accepted, knowing when to give "the right response."

Vidal has amplified Ammianus Marcellinus' account of the incident to show that Julian, like every politician, was an artful dodger. When one of the soldiers demanded he wear a diadem, he simply said he had none; when someone suggested he borrow his wife's, Julian again had the right response: " 'You don't want an emperor who wears a woman's jewels' " (p. 257). Finally a standard-bearer made a circlet from the battered chain of the regimental eagle and crowned him Julian Augustus.

As Vidal said in the Goldwater interview, "politics is improvisation"; and so was Julian's life—an improvisation on the theme of Man, with the appropriate mask and dialogue for each sketch. He played all his roles superbly —the threatened child, the dispassionate catechist, the devotee of the mystery religions, the champion of religious toleration who would not tolerate Christians teaching Greek literature, and finally the visionary who thought he was the incarnation of Alexander the Great.

Julian almost reached thirty-three, the age at which Alexander (not to mention Jesus Christ) died. The circumstances of Julian's death will always be a mystery. Following Libanius, who maintained he was killed by a Christian in his own army, Vidal exercised the prerogative of the historical novelist and gave the murderer a name—Callistus, Julian's bodyguard and, of course, a fervent believer in Christ.

In *Messiah* and *Julian*, religion encourages man's desire to become God and then deserts him at the moment of apotheosis. Cavesword and Julian's paganism began nobly—the one attempting to deliver man from fear of death, the other to free him from the restrictions of a universal religion. Instead, each created an atmosphere of fanaticism and superstition that completely negated its humanistic end. Both shared one common feature— syncretism; neither was a pure religion, if indeed there ever was such a phenomenon. Both systems proved that opposites resist reconciliation. When Plato's *Republic* is amalgamated with the Sermon on the Mount or when Neoplatonism is forced to mate with Mithraism, each strain fights to preserve its individuality and balks at forming a stable union. But one element always gains supremacy, and historically, whether for good or ill, it was Christianity.

Legend has it that Julian died with an admission of defeat: "Thou hast conquered, O Galilean!" But these last words of the Apostate were probably an invention of the fifth-century Christian historian Theodoret. And yet the Galilean did conquer; or rather the powerful myths he embodied triumphed over the Church's denial of their existence.

8

The Political Animal

In 1945, VIDAL told Anaïs Nin that one day he would become President of the United States; in 1972, he told an interviewer that no one of his generation was better qualified for the position: "And I could have made it, too —if it hadn't been for this fag thing."[1]

One seriously doubts that the "fag thing" had much to do with the dream deferred, or—given the state of American politics today—with the dream never to be realized. If voters were puzzled by the fact that Eugene McCarthy traveled with a copy of More's *Utopia*, they would hardly accept a candidate who claimed he was closer to Petronius than to any other writer.

However, in 1960 Vidal did run for Congress as the Democratic-Liberal candidate in New York's classically conservative twenty-ninth district, comprising the coun-

ties of Dutchess, Ulster, Greene, Columbia, and Scho-
harie. When he first announced his intention to run for
the House, he was not taken seriously. But Vidal never
entered a new medium without achieving some success
in it, and what may have begun as a lark developed into
a model campaign.

It was not easy to run against the Republican candidate, J. Ernest Wharton, who had been in the House of
Representatives for ten years. Vidal had difficulty getting press coverage unless it was to the advantage of his
opponent; and when a local paper decided to back him,
the Republican leaders of the community suddenly
stopped advertising in it. Undaunted, he campaigned
from one end of the district to the other, often supported
by Paul Newman and Joanne Woodward. For the sake
of convention, he memorized the Pledge of Allegiance,
which he had never learned at boarding school; but the
incantation to Old Glory was one of his few concessions
to protocol. When it was time for taking a position, Vidal
did not resort to equivocation. Believing that gifted students should be assisted with state and federal grants, he
advocated federal aid to education—an explosive issue in
the district, where it was considered unconstitutional—
and even suggested lotteries as a source of educational
funding. Although Vidal lost the election by 23,000 votes,
it was the closest contest the district had had since 1910.
So perhaps he was justified in terming it "a victorious
defeat."

While 1960 ended with a victorious defeat at the polls,
it began with an unqualified success on Broadway. On
March 31, *The Best Man* opened for a run of 520 performances. Vidal knew exactly what Broadway wanted in
a presidential year: a skillfully constructed play center-

ing about a familiar political trio—the man of conscience, the man of appeasement, and the man of the
people—whose identities would provide material for
open-ended debate long after the third-act curtain had
fallen. The intellectual is William Russell, a former
Secretary of State with a mild case of satyriasis. With
Melvyn Douglas in the role, one thought immediately of
Dean Acheson, whom he resembled physically; yet
when Douglas spoke, his inflections seemed to be those
of Adlai Stevenson. Furthermore, Russell's extramarital
affairs recalled the old stories about Warren G. Harding.
Russell was a composite of all these men and thus was
none of them; just when his dossier appeared to be complete, Vidal inserted an addendum—a medical history
that could easily be exaggerated to prove mental instabil-
ity.

The opportunist is Senator Joe Cantwell, a television
crime-fighter, a believer in God, and a faithful spouse.
Could he be Joe McCarthy or perhaps Estes Kefauver?
The role was played by Frank Lovejoy, whose Nixon-
like appearance provided a third possibility. With Lee
Tracy impersonating Art Hockstader, the last of the
Hick Presidents, the model was indisputable—Harry
Truman, the Great Hick himself. But Hockstader died
at the end of Act II, damning both Russell and Cantwell;
as a middle-of-the-roader who was neither an egghead
nor a scoundrel, Hockstader could even have been modeled after Senator Gore.

In his Goldwater essay, Vidal warned commentators
never to impute subtlety to politicians, because they
have none; in *The Best Man*, he applied his own principle.
The fight for the Presidency is rough and dirty; Cantwell
divulges the details of Russell's mental history, and Rus-

sell acquires information that could link Cantwell to a homosexual ring he allegedly exposed during the war by trapping his roommate *in flagrante delicto*. Like *Visit to a Small Planet*, *The Best Man* is reaching the nightmare stage when Russell finally withdraws his candidacy, releasing his delegates with instructions that they support an unknown, Governor John Merwin.

Again the god descended from the machine with a ready solution. By setting the play during a convention, Vidal was implicitly asking the audience to "elect" either Cantwell or Russell. The average voter will not tolerate an opportunist (although he has often had to); but the alternative is the intellectual who weighs his words so carefully that the country may collapse from his inability to find *le mot juste*. Instead, everyone hopes for the best man, that messianic unknown, who is discovered as coincidentally as a starlet in a drugstore. And it is precisely because he is an unknown that one naïvely believes he will be the golden mean between compromise and conscience.

The summer after the New York premiere of *The Best Man*, another of Vidal's political plays was produced, this time in stock. Originally entitled *Knife to the Hilt*, it is now known as *On the March to the Sea*;[2] the play was a dramatization of a 1956 television script, "Honor," a pseudo-Faulknerian melodrama about a *nouveau riche* Georgian and his pursuit of the frayed classical virtues the South had transplanted from old Rome. John Hinks, an ex-miller, acquired the worst qualities of the Petronian parvenu by amassing enough wealth to make himself the equal of the Southern landowners. While the Civil War was raging, he built a mansion and sent his sons off to battle, all in the name of honor.

Hinks' concept of honor was peculiarly Roman in its pragmatism. Honor was not a speculative virtue but a dynamic one that took on substance and form through action:

It is what you *do* that makes you what you are, not what you say, not even what you think. It is what you do in the world. The thing you *have* to do because something tells you inside: *that* is honour.

—*On the March to the Sea,* I,i

This notion of honor was strikingly similar to Art Hockstader's view of power, which was also an active pursuit, not an abstract entity:

Now I am here to tell you this: power is not a toy we give to good children; it is a weapon and the strong man takes it and he uses it and I can assure you he don't turn it on himself nor let another man come at him with a knife, that he don't fight back.

—*The Best Man,* II,iii

As political virtues, power and honor are so synonymous that a man can cultivate one to achieve the other. But when these virtues leave the world of essences and harden into human acts, they often become morally ambiguous: a man can sacrifice his sons for honor or his country for power. Hinks' "honor" is as ambiguous as Hockstader's "power"; yet the politician must pursue both to the hilt as if he were testing a knife to see how deep it can penetrate.

On the March to the Sea was produced professionally in Bonn, Germany in 1961, but never on Broadway. As a gloss on *The Best Man,* it is good collateral reading; as a play, it is best described by its subtitle, "A Southron Tragedy."

Vidal's next project was the Broadway adaptation of Friedrich Duerrenmatt's parable of the fall of Rome, *Romulus the Great*. He was attracted to the play because it reflected his own view of imperialism; but *Romulus the Great* was also Vidal's kind of drama, where a situation inexorably ascended the pyramid of tragedy, reversed direction at the top, and tumbled down into the open arms of a *deus ex machina*.

Although *Romulus* (1962), as the adaptation was called, did not have a lengthy run in New York, it typified Vidal's concept of theatre better than any of his other plays. Following the classical theory that drama should teach as well as delight, Vidal deliberately softened his didacticism with a wit that made his dark vision bearable. He also cheated his audience the way Euripides did: by summoning a *deus ex machina* to complete an action that humans began but could not resolve.

Romulus exhibits this tension between the logical and the irrational. On the eve of Rome's fall in 476 A.D., Romulus Augustulus, the last of the Caesars, breeds chickens and spouts aphorisms as his world crumbles. With a nonchalant wave of a bejeweled hand, he dismisses the news of the Goths' advances, preferring to concentrate on his chickens, whose productivity is rewarded with titles like "Savior of the State." There is a method to Romulus' madness; like many a politician, he prefers to do nothing in time of crisis. Actually, he wants Rome to fall so he can liquidate an empire that has betrayed its mission to mankind. Rome is simply too corrupt to save.

While it has become painfully common to compare the Roman Empire with the United States, there is one similarity that has nothing to do with the overworked analogy of moral decline. Students of classical history think of Rome between 510 and 42 B.C. as a republic *(res publica)*. In theory, it was; in practice, Rome was an oligarchy dominated by the Senate. Even the so-called principate was an Oriental-Hellenistic monarchy where the Emperor, or *princeps* as he called himself, took over the magistracies of the republic and consolidated their functions in himself, becoming consul, high priest, and wielder of the tribunician power simultaneously. Technically, the republic and the principate were both unconstitutional, for they had subverted their own ends.

Vidal came to a similar conclusion about America. After researching *Julian* and studying Suetonius' *Lives of the Caesars*, he began writing about the "American Empire" instead of the "American Republic." Vidal believed that to avoid anarchy, the United States adopted Caesarism and willed its destiny "to be the last empire on earth."³ Beany, the Senator's son in *Weekend* (1968), returns from Europe denouncing the "predatory empire" that pretended to be a peace-loving republic. And empires, as Vidal has warned on the talk shows and at the end of *An Evening with Richard Nixon and* . . . (1972), are difficult to abandon once they are acquired.

Romulus had no difficulty dissolving his empire because there was nothing to dissolve but a name. In moralistic cinema, the empire collapses while a volcano spills out lava, a fitting symbol for the spiritual viscosity of the age. But *Romulus* is not *The Last Days of Pompeii* (1935). When the Emperor meets the barbarian Ottaker for a high-level talk, he discovers, to his amazement (and the audience's), that the Goth is also a dedicated chicken-breeder. Rome ends with neither a bang nor a whimper, but with a cackle. Romulus liquidates his empire, or rather he entrusts it to the barbarians while he retires, the newly styled King of Italy, to spend the rest of his days with his chickens. Romulus has lived out the dream-fantasy of any American who was terrified by his country's growing imperialism: he dissolved the empire without disrupting either the course of history or the activities of the people. *Triste dictu*, an act of liquidation that injures no one, particularly the Muse of History, can only occur in the land of Nod where the action of *Romulus* transpires.

Romulus was a financial failure, but *Julian* (1964) remained on the best-seller list for over eight months. Next came *Washington, D.C.* (1967), a novel Vidal had to write, if only to prove what young Peter Sanford said as he imagined himself speaking in epigrammatic brilliance before HUAC: " 'Politics is the only profession in which mediocrities can gain the world's attention through slander.' "[4] One might also add that the political novel is the only form of fiction in which mediocrities can slander with impunity because the genre not only grants them the right, but also dignifies them with the title of Machiavels. A novel about political machinations is as predictable as a play about the theatre; each confirms what we already know. One expects to find the mighty toppling through liquor and sex, careers ending abruptly with the disclosure of some ancient secret, the young Turks battling the old guard, the devious protégé eclipsing, if not annihilating, his unsuspecting patron—in short, the customary types who weave bastardy or bitchery, depending upon the dominance of testosterone or estrogen.

The world of *Washington, D.C.* is so archetypal with its Wise Old Men and Young Princes that it seems to have been carved out of the collective unconscious; it is a world so bloated with canapés and watercress sandwiches that Peter Sanford's expanding waistline becomes a metaphor for the mental obesity of Capitol Hill. Everything conforms so perfectly to our preconceived notions that we keep shaking our heads—not out of ennui, for it is hardly a boring book—but from endless agreement. It is an undeniably familiar universe, created for the old believers who have seen the phantoms of the past return to envelop political hopefuls in their baneful ectoplasm. Yet for all its eerie familiarity, *Washington, D.C.* far surpasses a novel like Allen Drury's *Advise and Consent* (1959) because of the parallels Vidal has drawn between politics, the Hollywood star system, and sexual domination, where the need to create idols for the public is matched by the desire for a plaything in bed.

The novel spans a period from 1937 to the mid-fifties and contrasts the fortunes of two families, the Sanfords and the Days; the one destined for success, the other for failure. Vidal had used poetic openings before, especially in *The Season of Comfort,* where one could almost smell the magnolia blossoms. In *Washington, D.C.,* Vidal also found his opening metaphor in nature—a summer storm with serpentine lightning uncoiling across a chaotic sky. Peter Sanford, who is sixteen but not foolish enough to sacrifice himself to the elements, takes cover in the family poolhouse where he discovers his sister and her lover on a rubber mattress.

It is not coincidental that lightning slithers across the sky while a woman's legs encircle her lover's; nor is it by chance that the storm abates at the moment of orgasm. This is Washington, D.C., 1937, an Eden soon to be dissolved by the forked lightning of war and aggression. The parallels with the *Book of Genesis* are unmistakable;

the earthly paradise ended when the serpent entered it, and the tranquillity of isolation ceased when a storm uncoiled like a snake while a modern Adam and Eve were tasting the forbidden fruit.

The Adam is Clay Overbury, who is so much of a gentleman (or else is in so much of a hurry) that he never removes his shoes and garters; his name is so loaded with symbolism (mold-mortician) that in retrospect it seems like overkill. His Eve, Enid Sanford, is Peter's sister; and the setting is Laurel House, on the Virginia side of the Potomac, the home of Blaise and Frederika Sanford, the newspaper tycoon and his mousy wife. Complementing the Sanfords are the Days: Senator James Burden Day, his wife Kitty, and their daughter Diana.

Washington, D.C. is so thickly populated with minor characters that occasionally they seem to take control of a story belonging primarily to Burden Day. When the novel moves away from him and into the grasp of Peter, Enid, Clay, or Blaise, it is only the supporting cast's momentary upstaging of the star whose return to center stage restores the drama to its proper focus. Day's career circumscribes a circle of tragic inevitability that in its gradual closure draws the lives of the others into a common center.

The inspiration for Burden Day was Senator Gore, Dean of the Right wing of the Democratic Party, who lost his seat in the Senate when he refused to support the New Deal. Vidal saw his grandfather as the prototype of the Ciceronian politician who, had he lumbered along in the Senate denouncing the liberals with Southern bombast, would merely be regarded as a crotchety isolationist. Yet it is intriguing to consider how a conservative would have fared if he had run for President on the eve of the Second World War. The similarities to Senator Gore obviously stop here; Vidal posed the question and from it came the novel. He selected the Senator's best qualities—conservatism, idealism, and a belief that politics can be a noble profession—and transferred them to the character of James Burden Day.

Toward the end of Chapter One, Burden Day encounters his serpent and his specter. In front of the Capitol, he is approached by Mr. Nillson, an oil man, who lacks the ability to be a politician and therefore finances the careers of others. Nillson's desire to manipulate Burden Day is not that different from Clay's desire to master Enid. Vidal had suggested a connection between sex and politics in *The Judgment of Paris*, where Regina's offer of power was accompanied by the offer of her body. In an unpublished and unproduced play, *The Ways of Love* (1955), which contained material that was later incorporated into *Washington, D.C.*, Vidal made a pointed comparison between the politician and the seducer: ". . . a politician is really nothing but a Don Juan. Instead of servicing ladies he services millions of voters."

Seduction can be physical or verbal. With Clay Overbury, it is the manipulation of his partner toward an orgasm that is aggressively one-sided. With Nillson, it is the need for vicarious power that is also achieved through a quasi-sexual act of entering the victim's psyche and reducing it to a private habitation.

In an effort to forget Nillson's offer to underwrite his presidential campaign, Burden Day retires to his favorite haunt near Bull Run to reminisce on the glory of the Old South. To his father's disgust, he admired the Confederacy and always lamented the fact that he was born too late to fight in the Civil War. But the site of his reverie is as serpentine as the lightning that presaged the end of isolationism at the opening of the novel: "Near Bull Run there was a field where Civil War earthworks twisted like a huge snake beneath tall grass" (p. 35). Soon an apparition visits him in the form of a Confederate soldier. It is his father disguised as the angel of death, the realist parent coming to haunt the romantic son whose ideals are now more antiquated than the Confederacy's.

While Burden Day would have given his life for the South, his father holds such patriotism in contempt. Yet Burden Day kept the bullet that struck his father at Shiloh; but after the apparition, he buried the talisman in the earth. The episode was modeled after a similar one in the life of Senator Gore, whose father was also wounded at Shiloh. As a boy, young Tom Gore had to swear on the bullet that he would remain faithful to populism and always remember the Civil War that divided the nation. When he disobeyed his father by running for the Senate as a Democrat, the sacred bullet became a piece of flattened metal that had lost its power to destroy.

The temptation and the apparition, occurring one after the other, foreshadow the decline of Burden Day. Since he never had a son, he anticipated marriage between his assistant Clay Overbury and his only child, Diana. But Clay knows the Senator is an anachronism and elopes with Enid Sanford, even at the risk of being disowned temporarily by her father. On the rebound, Diana marries a socialist with a wooden leg. Burden Day's fall is almost as swift as his rise. On the eve of Pearl Harbor, he experiences a double defeat: he is excluded from a special meeting with the President; and as he leaves the Senate, he sees in the shadows the figure of an old Senator returning to his lonely hotel room and his yellowed copies of the *Congressional Record*. The new regime has rejected Burden Day, and the old is merely a grotesque reflection of himself.

While the Year King prepares for the inevitable interment, the rival awaits his inheritance; as Burden Day declines, Clay Overbury rises. The estrangement between Clay and his father-in-law is only temporary. After Clay becomes a war hero, Sanford, who must create idols to justify an existence that is unworthy of veneration, recants and maps out his son-in-law's new career. When Burden Day decides to run again for the Senate, he discovers that Clay has similar plans. The former legislative assistant, now the usurper, threatens to make public a recording of an old telephone conversation that would implicate Burden Day in one of Nillson's shady land sales.

Sensing the end, the Senator returns to his favorite hill, only to discover it has become a construction site. Eager for contact with any vestige of the old order, he drives to a slave cabin by the Potomac. This is presumably the cabin where Jim and Bob spent their weekend of awakening in *The City and the Pillar*. In the earlier novel, it was a symbol of the end of innocence; in *Washington, D.C.*, the decaying frames and the contraceptive-cluttered floor suggest the kind of world Burden Day is leaving. Again the Confederate soldier appears, looking exactly as he did at the Battle of Shiloh—rifle in hand and blood dripping from a shoulder wound. Burden Day admits his failure to his father's ghost: " 'You were right. . . . It has all gone wrong. You should be pleased' " (p. 346). After he tries desperately to stop the flow of blood from his father's wound, he embraces the specter and both fall into the Potomac—the two orders finally reconciled in a death lock.

Most tragedies are poetic constructs, and the cosmic questions they ask reverberate long after the curtain has fallen. But only in tragedy is there the peculiar ambiguity of defeat tempered with victory. In trying to close the wound that was left gaping since the Civil War, Burden Day falls to his death—a suicide to those who would consider any attempt at reconciliation as suicidal, a triumphant rebirth to those who believe the heroic spirit is immune to mortality. Burden Day has triumphed like the kings of tragedy: by dying and being reborn as myth.

Washington, D.C. was more than a delineation of a society the author knew intimately. It was an attempt to define a period when the country discovered its mission like the ape who learned it could kill with its ancestors' bones. For Peter Sanford, the bombing of Pearl Harbor became a series of frames where his *kudos* would be immortalized in movie houses throughout the world. For the anti-Communists, World War II was only a struggle with Japan: " 'If we help Hitler with Russia, *he'll* help us with the Japanese' " (p. 167). With the end of the war and the extinction of the twin scapegoats, the public clamored for another ogre. This time it was Communism, and the prewar left-wingers became McCarthyites who testified against their Bolshevik friends.

What is so fascinating about these characters who are continually undergoing political metamorphosis is their total lack of gender. One accepts the fact that the males are men and the females women as if it were a noble lie. But their sex is ritual combat; and their lives, the ascent up the ladder of preferment. They have achieved a kind of disemboweled essence from playing the game to the letter and conforming to the unwritten law that the politician is promiscuous while his wife is monogamous. By plying themselves with watercress sandwiches, they became as unsubstantial as hors d'oeuvre; and by allowing the totem father to groom his favorite son for the dream career, they turned the doctrine of succession into a steer-judging contest.

It is in the patron-protégé relationship that Vidal has made one of his most frightening suggestions: at the core of such patronage is homosexuality denied. Enid outrages her father when she explains his peculiar alliance with Clay in terms of unnatural love: " 'After all, Clay will do anything to help his career. That's why he let you fall in love with him . . .' " (p. 266).

Patronage is a necessary evil that is only tolerable if the patron realizes his secondary role in the fostering of talent. When patronage takes the form of frustrated fatherhood, it can easily become seduction if the protégé is pliable, rape if he is recalcitrant. Enid is only partially correct when she accuses her father and husband of being lovers. Blaise and Clay could never be true lovers because they are incapable of love. They can only use each other in the political equivalent of mutual masturbation. The homosexual pattern they display in their relationship is as loveless and sterile as the courting ceremony in Plato's Athens where the old lover would write formally correct but poetically lifeless verses to the boy who caught his fancy. The courting was seduction reduced to the niceties of style. Vidal's conception of political patronage is the ultimate locker-room trip where the young hopeful flexes his muscles and the buyer waits for the ripple. Significantly, when they are undressing in the poolhouse, Blaise studies Clay's body until he blushes. Prize candidate or prize stud, it's all the same.

What also distinguishes *Washington, D.C.* from other political novels is the correlation Vidal makes between politics and the movies. He sees little difference between the convention halls and the Hollywood soundstages, or for that matter, between politicians and movie stars. His essay "The Twenty-Ninth Republican Convention" (1968) is more film review than convention coverage. Ronald Reagan of the dyed hair and "porcelain-capped teeth" seems to have stepped out of "some shining Carverville where good Lewis Stone forever lectures Andy Hardy on the virtues of thrift and the wisdom of the contract system at Metro-Goldwyn-Mayer."[5] Rockefeller's "upper class tough boy accent" recalls Montgomery Clift's in *The Heiress;* and Nixon's rouser ("Let's win this one for Ike!") is a football cheer from *Knute Rockne.*

In *Washington, D.C.,* Clay Overbury becomes a national hero through the purple prose of ex-film critic Harold Griffiths, who covers the war the same way he reviews movies. Next, Clay's life is turned into a film biography that depicts the heroic acts he never performed in the service. Griffiths, who idolizes movie stars so much that he closes doors like Kay Francis, creates an Audie Murphy out of an opportunist.

There is little difference between the political columnists who make a provincial city into the American Rome and the syndicated gossips who turn Hollywood into the American Eldorado. Griffiths manages to work both sides of the one-way street. Politicians and movie stars are mythic creations designed to fill the vacancies in a pantheon that no longer commands belief; they embody the American dream of arriving at the White

House from a log cabin or arriving at MGM from a drugstore counter. Each requires fantasy experts to pluck the eyebrows or elongate the mouth, choose the wardrobe and the scripts, hush up a private affair or publicize a rival's. And in the final analysis, campaign speeches differ from scenarios only to the extent that bombast differs from the vernacular, each being an extreme of the commonplace.

Although Vidal has described Washington, D.C., as an empire of moguls, he does not deny that at least in theory politics can be a noble endeavor. Burden Day's favorite quotation comes from Plato's *Ninth Letter*:

Each of us is born not for himself alone. We are born partly for our country, partly for our friends. The various contingencies that overtake our lives also make many demands upon us. When our country herself calls us to public life, it would perhaps be strange not to respond, since one must otherwise at the same time give place to worthless men who do not enter public life for the best motives. (p. 73)

But the *Letter* was spurious, as Peter reminded his grandfather before his death. Still, for a work of dubious authorship, the sentiments are sublime.

The success Vidal had enjoyed during the sixties with *The Best Man* (the play and the film), *Julian*, and *Washington, D.C.* ended with *Weekend* (1968), his third "quadrennial" offering. Vidal believed it was his mission to contribute something dramatic to each presidential year, on the assumption that the conventions were inadequate sources of theatre. In 1960 there was *The Best Man*, followed four years later by the screen version; in 1968, he offered *Weekend*. Vidal was clearly hoping for another Broadway hit; like *The Best Man*, *Weekend* opened in

March, but not for a run of 520 performances. It lasted less than three weeks.

Weekend was a total miscalculation. In a less radicalized age, it might have enjoyed a modest run; but Vietnam had left its impact on the stage, and a "quiet" political comedy could no longer attract an audience. The West Side liberals, who then were divesting themselves of any intellectual accoutrements they might have acquired through education, wanted blood, not banter. The fun had gone out of politics, and *Weekend* closed after twenty-one performances.

Weekend also contains no surprises. The idea of a presidential candidate's son coming home to Rock Creek Park with his black fiancée might have been novel if a similar gimmick had not been used in the 1967 movie *Guess Who's Coming to Dinner*. In the film, the sexes were reversed: the white liberal was female, and her black fiancé was a distinguished scientist. But the "Guess Who?" game is common to both William Rose's film script and Vidal's play; and so is the contrast between the liberated black and his (her) unemancipated parents.

Since Vidal was now living the life of a Rome-based expatriate, he saw as vices what most Americans would regard merely as incongruities. Consequently, there is not a decent character in *Weekend*. The young and the old keep blackmailing each other until there is no other way to resolve the action except to haul out the gods, this time in the guise of an opinion poll indicating that most voters would accept a President whose daughter-in-law is black.

His fourth quadrennial play, *An Evening with Richard Nixon and . . .* (1972), was also unsuccessful and survived for a mere seventeen performances exclusive of previews. Several months prior to the April 30 opening, the text appeared in the bookstores under the title *An Evening with Richard Nixon*, a reconstruction of the career of the thirty-seventh President largely from his own words.[6] The source of each quotation is documented in scholarly fashion in case the skeptics refuse to believe Nixon once said, "If elected [Governor of California] I promise the best Communist control of any state." While economy of expression is commendable in campaign speeches, it often leads to obscurity of thought or what the grammarians used to call a "howler."

Vidal conceived the play as a political vaudeville emceed by George Washington, with Dwight D. Eisenhower as the comedian in baggy pants (fitting attire for a golfer) and John Kennedy as the petulant end man. Although the setting is never specified, it is clearly the afterlife (limbo or hell, depending on where one places former politicians), a spectral Grover's Corners where yesterday's chiefs of state can peruse the current President's book of life and marvel at its lack of infinite variety.

On Broadway, the play was called *An Evening with Richard Nixon and . . .* ; Vidal thought the ellipsis was necessary because the radical liberals would not be interested in spending two hours with Nixon alone. The provocative three dots suggested alternatives, no less cartoon-like but perhaps less boring, such as Harry Truman, Nikita Khrushchev, Gloria Steinem, and Martha Mitchell. But the radicals were also unimpressed with the supporting cast, who apparently were not worth a ten dollars top.

In the revised version that was presented at the Shubert Theatre, the play opened with a prologue; two commentators, Pro and Con, presumably William F. Buckley, Jr., and Vidal himself,[7] were enthroned on swivel chairs and debating (what else?) Richard Nixon's merits or lack of them. When their debate reached an impasse, they literally dissolved into the smoky air of the underworld where Washington, Eisenhower, and Kennedy assumed control of the evening—the classic case of the dead rushing in where the living fear to tread. Like the judges of Hades, they examined and occasionally commented on Nixon's life as it unfolded before their court.

The device is old hat, both for the theatre and for Vidal. Aristophanes employed a similar motif in *The Frogs*, where Dionysus descends to Hades and judges a debate between Aeschylus and Euripides. Aristophanes reproduced the styles of the two tragedians by having them speak as they wrote—Aeschylus in exotic metaphor, Euripides in monotonous realism. However, Vidal completely ignored mimesis and made Nixon speak the words he had actually uttered. In Vidal's own play *A Drawing Room Comedy* (1970), which has not yet been produced in New York, a character dies early in the evening and spends the rest of it in the hell of repetition, like Sartre's trio in *No Exit*. *Richard Nixon* also owes something to Act III of Thornton Wilder's *Our Town*, where Emily returns from the dead to spend one day among the living, speaking and hearing only what was spoken and heard on Tuesday, February 11, 1899.

In *The Frogs*, *A Drawing Room Comedy*, *No Exit*, and *Our Town*, the dead speak *from* the grave, while in *Richard Nixon*, the President speaks *to* it. By bringing Nixon before a ghostly tribunal where he can only repeat what he had said publicly (there was some invented dialogue printed in darker type in the Random House edition),

Vidal was subjecting him to a premature day of judgment which might be his perverse way of either questioning the President's existence or of suggesting that a politician's exterior vitality conceals a dead soul.

Vidal has been accused of quoting Nixon out of context. When the President said, "California cannot afford to stand pat," the line became a thoughtless slur against the First Lady, Thelma (Pat) Nixon. While quoting out of context is not the highest form of humor, it was part of Vidal's attempt to reveal the hidden meanings that often lurk behind a politician's clichés. But the attempt backfired; in constructing a play out of Nixon's own words, Vidal gave the President's statements the semblance of order as well as the dignity of dialogue. The evening evolved into a mosaic where fragments of verbatim quotes arranged themselves like pieces of multicolored glass. The symmetry was dazzling, and many people left the theatre arguing that for the first time Richard Nixon actually made sense.

And they were correct; when ambiguities multiply, they negate each other and produce models of false clarity. All any politician needs is someone to connect his disjointed ideas and arrange them in sequence; so while there is no real progression of thought, there seems to be one because the ideas acquire a beginning, a middle, and an end. Of course, few realized the beginning and the end were the same and the middle was illusory.

Admirers of Nixon, if indeed any attended the play during its two-week run, could hardly object to Vidal's method. The evening was no more vicious than the "Friars' Roast" or the kangaroo courts during centennial celebrations. In *Weekend*, everyone is a conspirator, but in *Richard Nixon* there is only one, and it is not the thirty-seventh President; it is America who has conspired against herself.

What begins as an evaluation of Richard Nixon ends with Washington's accusing Eisenhower and Kennedy of turning the Republic into an Empire. In allowing the former Presidents to defend themselves against Washington's charge, Vidal has honored the traditional rights of the dead, which are as old as Book XI of Homer's *Odyssey;* having acquired the self-knowledge they lacked in life, the dead can now explain themselves to the living without sophistry.

Ike responds to the accusation by invoking the laws of history:

General, we deal with such a small space of history at a time —things are in motion when we arrive—so, like it or not we have to move *with* events. Some of us keep the peace better than others, but nothing more. Anyway, you came at the beginning. You were lucky. We came at the . . . we came later in the story. (p. 132)

And Kennedy, whom Washington had denounced earlier as a man "entirely governed by self-love," is given the most important speech in the play:

I wanted a just society but I thought it could not be done if we gave up our empire, and empires, no matter how achieved, are dangerous things to let go. (p. 132)

Finally, "A Colonial" drags the branch of a cherry tree across the stage and poses the same question he asked when the curtain rose: "George, who cut down that cherry tree?" Kennedy immediately blames Nixon; but

Ike, who saw life steadily, if not whole, answers for the country: "We . . . uh, we all did!"

As the curtain fell, the national anthem erupted from a loudspeaker in its hideously familiar orchestration—all brass and no strings. For all its cabaret satire, *Richard Nixon* ended with a mass *mea culpa*, and one left the Shubert Theatre the way one leaves an Irish wake. The joviality lasts until the cold air of mortality nips the face, and suddenly there is the realization that the grave is a little closer than it was before.

Richard Nixon is important not so much for what it says about America as for what it reveals about the author. It could only have been written by someone who felt too deeply about his country to allow it to pursue a predatory course with impunity. Since Vidal had inherited his grandfather's isolationism, he understood that empires "are dangerous things to let go," but did not know how to dissolve them except by literary means, like a dream or a *deus ex machina*.

But there is no god on wires in *Richard Nixon*. The entire play was a *cri de coeur* caught at the stage where it could easily become a guffaw by the expansion of the right facial muscles. The masks of comedy and tragedy had been interchanged so frequently during the evening that at the end one did not know if he had witnessed a bloodletting or a blood transfusion; both do more than prick the surface. Theatre historians can decide whether *Richard Nixon* is Aristophanic burlesque or Theatre of Fact. In the meantime, what the eponymous hero of Orson Welles' *Citizen Kane* (1941) said of himself is equally true of Gore Vidal: "I am, have been, and will be only one thing—an American."

9

Myra of the Movies;
Or, the Magnificent
Androgyne

VIDAL'S NOVELS often resemble film scripts, with their
dissolves, cuts, and cheery sunbursts before the last fade-
out. Because the conventional film represents the daylight dream, it has a structure that loosely parallels, in
Aristotelian terms, "life as it *ought* to be." Within that
"ought," the probable becomes the possible; and the possible, the necessary. Literary critics envision fiction as
either pyramidic or circular; a similar case can be made
for film, which can assume the form of a pyramid rising
wondrously from a shaky foundation to a transcendent
apex, or a circle miraculously completing the curve life
leaves unclosed.

"In the decade between 1935 and 1945, no irrelevant
film was made in the United States. During those years,
the entire range of human (which is to say, American)

legend was put on film, and any profound study of those extraordinary works is bound to make crystal-clear the human condition."[1] Thus argued Myra Breckinridge, who was so convinced of her thesis that she ranked the films of the forties higher than the works of Shakespeare.

Ludicrous? To littérateurs, but not to Myra. The era she admired will best be remembered for its confusion of the ordinary with the archetypal. G.I.s became Achillean heroes; faithful housewives, Penelopes; pubescent enlistees, questers; a hamlet in Middle America, an Everytown; and Lon McCallister, an Everyman. The forties were the Golden Age of the American cinema, not in the sense that they were the apogee of art, but of myth —a distinction Myra never made.

United by a patriotism that unfurled itself in frames of red, white, and blue, film makers of the forties discovered, without benefit of Lévi-Strauss or Rollo May, a fundamental truth about civilizations: they last only as long as the myths on which they are founded. Hollywood created the myth of a country asleep in a post-Depression slumber, suddenly awakened by Pearl Harbor. We became a nation fighting "Krauts" (sometimes referred to even less euphemistically as "Heinies") and "shifty-eyed Japs," as the *Batman* serial called the enemy. America rallied as never before, and out of its renewal came the mythical figures of Rosie the Riveter, Sadsack, Kilroy, Willie and Joe, and a host of anomalous types— the undraftable flag-wavers turning to defense work, wallflowers burgeoning at the Stage Door Canteen, the boys who danced their last jitterbug before shoving off for "destination unknown," the girls who waited, and the girls who didn't.

The *dramatis personae* of the war years were all happily

immortalized on celluloid—"*blessed* celluloid" as Myra called it. But it was Apollonian celluloid (to use Nietzsche's distinction) rather than Dionysian: the epic vision as distinguished from the tragic. To Nietzsche, the Apollonian world found its fullest expression in Homer's pantheon of earth-shaking gods and ox-eyed goddesses who dined on ambrosia and bled ichor. The Olympians were more durable versions of ourselves, performing our small-scaled actions with an operatic flourish.

And so were the celluloid Olympians, those vegetation deities always dying and being reborn, killed off in one epic and resurrected in another. In addition to the warriors who bled ketchup on Iwo Jima, there were the nimbus-crowned gods and goddesses on the home front. The Hollywood hagiographers canonized everyone; hookers became Broadway Babies, vulgar but virginal; homosexuals were dandies with boutonnieres; and the castrating female, a career woman whose attire (pin-striped suit and pumps) bore a slight but not suspicious resemblance to a male's. And the very thought that Lana Turner or Bette Davis defecated would be punishable in a circle of hell even Dante could not imagine.

Myra Breckinridge knew that this Apollonian veneer concealed a reality too awesome for most moviegoers to accept. Who, for example, was M. J. as played by Joan Crawford in *They All Kissed the Bride* (1942), the Boss Lady in her shirtwaist, tie, and suspenders who bullied the men in the firm? Who was this female executive with the masculine initials, grasping the arms of her swivel chair and crying out at her male underlings: "Why am I surrounded by such incompetence?" On the surface, M. J. was just a woman doing a man's job as the exigencies of World War II erased the line of demarcation, however temporarily, between the sexes. But Myra would see her as an androgyne who, to succeed in a man's profession, must first conquer her male competitors through ritual submission or—dare one say it?—symbolic rape.

However, Myra did not come unaided to her belief that the film shot by the camera was only the covering for the film shot by the unconscious. In 1947, Parker Tyler, a New Orleans-born poet-critic, published a book called *Magic and Myth of the Movies* that opened up those hidden chambers beneath the celluloid where the fantasist could find the script the scenarist *didn't* write. Myra so admired *Magic and Myth* that she yearned to write a study called *Parker Tyler and the Films of the Forties; or The Transcendental Pantheon.* In fact, Vidal's original title for the novel was *I Hated Parker Tyler:* "I needed an idol for Myra, and couldn't help thinking of Tyler. I used to read his criticism and howl."

Tyler's theories can indeed produce howls from anti-Freudians or, for that matter, from anyone who takes a dim view of myth criticism. Only the most devoted Frazerite would regard Veronica Lake of the peekaboo bang as a female Wotan, or the comedian braving the front lines as a medicine man endangering his life for the community. While most moviegoers considered *My Friend Flicka* (1943) as a sentimental tale of a boy and his horse and *The Outlaw* (1943) as a boobs n' bullets Western, Tyler viewed them as primitive rituals where the adolescent was initiated into totemism and homosexuality. If Flicka was a phallic symbol, what, might one ask, was Roy Rogers' relationship to Trigger?

Tyler was outrageous, but so was Myra; hence their affinity. Both of them understood that during the forties the Hollywood scenarist was restricted by criteria imposed by the Breen Office and pressure groups like the Legion of Decency. Script writers knew that explicit sexuality would offend a public that wanted Andy Hardy's innocence for its sons and Corliss Archer's naïveté for its daughters. But script writers could not slough off the influence of Freud; consequently, they took over the findings of psychology and reduced them to a mythic substratum which they buried in the hollows of the script. Myra, partly a Tylerian and partly a Dantean (she knew at least two levels of interpretation—the literal and the allegorical) managed to remove the overlay and find "the heart of light."

Tyler assumed the films of the forties worked from a double vision. If there were two films, then there must be two plots—one existing in the order of intention, the plot the scenarist wanted to write; the other existing on the printed page, the plot the Breen Office required of him. Both plots or *muthoi*, as Aristotle would have called them, coalesced so harmoniously that only a discerning moviegoer could separate them without disrupting the scenario's unity. Myra Breckinridge was such a moviegoer; in fact, she was the ultimate moviegoer. Once she learned, as she did from Tyler, how to separate the two plots, she could inhabit the scenario's nether world and live out the fantasies the script obliquely suggested.

Consequently, Myra would never see the Joan Crawford career woman as the female executive breaking her incipient balls to rise to the top of a man's profession. She would regard her as a rapist, subjecting her male employees to the same degradation that men forced upon women throughout the ages. If rape is man's ultimate humiliation of woman, it can also be woman's ultimate humiliation of man. Give Boss Lady a swivel chair, a dictaphone, and a pencil-scepter and she immediately becomes androgynous—tailored suit, upswept hair, and a bellowing Max Factor mouth. Give her a dildo and she acquires the appendage nature forgot to supply. When Myra rapes Rusty, he submits with the same combined masochism and trepidation that M. J.'s male lackeys exhibited in *They All Kissed the Bride*. Literally or symbolically, ravishment is ravishment. Myra was merely applying the principle of *reductio ad absurdum* to those "lady executive" comedies of the forties. She accomplished what M. J. only dreamed of doing.

What Myra's unconscious found in the films of the forties would seem reprehensible only to those who never read *Magic and Myth*, a work that received the endorsement of Eric Bentley, Marshall McLuhan, and Henry Miller among others. Tyler, who does not even possess a B.A., acquired the reputation in England for being something of a psychiatrist because he drew so heavily on Frazer, Freud, and Jung. Sinatra was "The Voice" discharging numen from his gangly frame. The determined lady who had no time for sex and her ardent pursuer who had world enough and time for it were variations of Diana and Endymion or Daphne and Apollo. The Wolf Man's eerie cry was the expression of his restless libido. Cary Grant as the drama critic in *Arsenic and Old Lace* (1944) would look for any opportunity to defer marriage to Priscilla Lane because he was afraid of getting a bad review in bed. Such were Tyler's theories. *Sic transit gloria*—perhaps. Still, he was the first to show how a somnolent generation reverted to paganism and worshiped what it dimly perceived.

Myra was fond of quoting *Magic and Myth* (always out of context), a practice Tyler deplored. In fact, he forbade any excerpts from the book to be used in the disastrous

1970 film version. Even Raquel Welch, the hypo-estro-genic Myra of the movie, lamented the removal of those "delicious raps of Parker Tyler." Nor did Vidal's belief that he did for Parker Tyler what Edward Albee did for Virginia Woolf close the wound. Myra was cinematically promiscuous; since she believed no irrelevant film was ever made in the forties, she embraced them all indiscriminately, extolling Tyler in the same breath with Phyllis Thaxter, Laraine Day, Betty Hutton, and other forgotten greats. Thus the younger cinemaphiles wondered if Tyler had become one of his own myths.

Meeting Parker Tyler is a session in demythologization. Somehow one expects a figure from a forties lobby card. The man not only exists, but he has also exorcised the ghosts of the past so successfully that he no longer hears their ululations. Myra would be shocked to see his luxury apartment in the West Village; there are no Bette Davis stills on the wall, no Andrews Sisters records on the floor. The forties lie submerged in the drift of sea shells scattered about his study. A copy of *Marius the Epicurean* lies open on a table, a reminder of his rarefied taste. His long silver hair has tried to form a peekaboo bang but only succeeded in effecting an innocuous wavelet. Even the neckerchief silently mocks Roy Rogers and the Sons of the Pioneers.

Tyler is quick to disclaim any responsibility for Myra's idolatry of *Magic and Myth* by stating firmly that he hated the forties, that he ridiculed the films of that era, and that his interest lay exclusively in their myths rather than in their nonexistent art. When asked who Myra Breckinridge is, Tyler will simply reply that if Flaubert could claim he was Madame Bovary, Gore Vidal must be Myra Breckinridge.

In *Screening the Sexes* (1972), Tyler, mellower and better

known because of the paperback editions of *The Hollywood Hallucination* and *Magic and Myth* (both of which
contain the same sympathetic introduction by Richard
Schickel), called the novel "a devastatingly flip satire"
and paid it a curious homage by commending the author's intentions and rapping his knuckles at the same
time:

> Vidal's book is a sexo-social satire that has its crudities. Yet it
> has its fine points, too, if one cares to look closely at today's
> erotic delusions-of-grandeur as they exist in the social mass.
> . . . Since the mass-myth is one to which, prior to Vidal, I have
> given a great deal of attention, it is not surprising that Vidal
> should have been inspired to make me Myra's muse. . . . I may
> be pardoned, then, for observing that Vidal deliberately gives
> a false idea of my book's tone and intentions by quoting from
> it only such sentences as seem solemn and academic, a little
> absurdly so out of context, and that what he is really being so
> self-conscious about is the tacit debt to my example.[2]

Myra's inspiration may have been Parker Tyler, but
Vidal courts a composite Muse. He is an intensely literary writer, borrowing freely and transforming his
sources through an age-old alchemy that T. S. Eliot
equated with maturity. One knew he must have been
reading the eighteenth-century novel before he wrote
The Judgment of Paris, with its "dear reader" asides. He
had also seen his share of science fiction films before
planning *Messiah. Myra Breckinridge* (1968), Tylerian as it
is, could only have been conceived by someone familiar
with the French New Novel, the ancient classics, and, of
course, the films of the forties.

The December 1967 *Encounter* contained one of Vidal's
finest essays, "French Letters: Theories of the New

Novel." It is not surprising that the following year *Myra* appeared, dealing a mortal blow to this strange art form of the fifties which was practiced and championed by Nathalie Sarraute, Alain Robbe-Grillet, Michel Butor, et al. The New Novel *(le roman nouveau)* dispenses with traditional methods of characterization and concentrates on inanimate objects to render as accurate a description of phenomena as possible. As a conventional novelist, Vidal is suspicious of the avant-gardism of the *roman nouveau:*

It is, however, a convention of the avant-garde that to be in advance of the majority is to be "right." But the New Novelists are not in advance of anyone. Their works derive from what they believe to be a need for experiment. . . . Yet in this they resemble everyone, since to have a liking for the new is to be with the dull majority.[3]

The New Novel was not produced by a literary parthenogenesis; its ancestor was Sartre's *Nausea* (1938), where Roquentin, contemptuous of a universe that is absurd and contingent, vomits out his disgust in a diary that is designed for self-therapy and, it would seem, for self-pity. Oddly enough, *Myra* is also a diary-novel. Can it be that Gore Vidal, pornographer-aesthete, was conversant enough with French literature to parody the existential *journal?*

On the advice of her dentist-psychiatrist, Dr. Montag, Myra maintains a diary to record "with an exact, literal sense . . . what it is like, from moment to moment, to be me . . ." (p. 5). Her diary spoofs Roquentin's self-conscious *journal* that was designed for exactly the same purpose: "Keep a diary to see clearly—let none of the nuances of small happenings escape even though they might seem to be nothing."[4] Roquentin records everything—his perception of an ink bottle, his confusion of a hand with a worm, the reflection of his face in a mirror, the blue shirt and purple suspenders of a bartender. Who knows what incident will become Ariadne's thread and extricate the self from the labyrinth of *angoisse?*

In itself, a diary like Roquentin's, composed of ink and tears and dried by a blotter that hardly absorbs the excess, is alternately tragic and comic. Of course, anyone who has had the "Nausea Blues" can empathize with Roquentin, for Existential Man, as we are told with unleavened seriousness, is ourself—the post-Hiroshima freak, the entropic wastelander, the solipsism—all the clichés with which the twentieth century defined us and which, in turn, we became. Yet nausea should also provoke laughter, as it apparently did with Iris Murdoch, who satirized Sartre's novel so magnificently in *Under the Net* (1954). If the prospect of an absurd universe can leave the mouth "sweetly disgusted," it can leave the ribs pleasantly convulsed. A contingent cosmos is hilarious, as Beckett's endearing tramps realized.

This is also Vidal's premise: the universe which most people see under the guise of film and through a lens darkly is absurd—hysterically so. But the New Novel is equally absurd; it replaces point of view with the camera eye that records things as they are because "things are *there*" and presumably people are not. Vidal will not bewail the camera's encroachments on the novel's domain; keening is shrill and undignified. Follow instead Maria's advice in *Twelfth Night* and "laugh yourself into stitches." Otherwise one becomes a bore.

Myra's diary is anything but boring, but Roquentin's is as humorless as a text in metaphysics. One of his major concerns is whether a sentence cast in the present becomes a thought of the past as soon as it is transcribed. If so, every story begins and ends with its opening sentence; and a diary, no matter how meticulously written, is merely the present decomposing into the past:

But everything changes when you talk about life; it's a change no one notices: the proof is that people talk about true stories. As if there could possibly be true stories; things happen one way and we tell about them in the opposite sense. (p. 57)

Myra's solution is simply to forget the beginning and start at the middle:

I shall not begin at the beginning since there is no beginning, only a middle into which you, fortunate reader, have just strayed, still uncertain as to what will be done to you in the course of our common voyage to my interior. (p. 6)

Roquentin is overwhelmed by the problem of existence: "I am. I am. I exist, I think, therefore I am: I am because I think, why do I think?" (p. 137). Myra scoffs at such gibberish: *"I know what I want and I know what I am"* (p. 135).

But what is Myra? She is simply everything she has seen and read. We know she has seen every film of the forties, but what has she read? She admits to studying the classics in translation at the New School, getting up the contemporary French novel on her own, and learning German to understand the films of the thirties. She is therefore familiar with Robbe-Grillet, whose "efforts to revive the novel as an art form are as ineffective as his attempts to destroy the art of film are successful" (p. 42). But Myra disliked Robbe-Grillet because he took the fun out of fiction; he was so preoccupied with things that in *Erasers* (1953) he lavished some of his best prose on the slicing of a tomato.

What Sartre and the New Novelists did with a deadly seriousness, Myra does with a giddy panache. For Myra Breckinridge, "whom no man will ever possess," can also wonder whether the present is the front of that double-edged blade called the past: "There is a crash outside my window—was a crash (in the time I took to write 'there is a crash' the tense changed)."

Myra also read Robbe-Grillet's *For a New Novel* (1963) and pondered his views on the world ("It *is*, quite simply"); objects ("things *are there*"); and metaphor ("contributes nothing new to the description"). Like a true *chosiste*, she maintains that "things are themselves entirely and do not need interpretation, only a minimal respect for their precise integrity" (p. 8). She is on the verge of comparing a splotch on her hotel wall to the scrotum viewed from behind, when she suddenly checks herself: "But no metaphors. Nothing is *like* anything else." Myra would like to be an ally of language, but the master has informed her that words can describe nothing precisely: "Is it possible to describe anything accurately? That is the problem set us by the French New Novelists. . . . I write that I 'care for' Mary-Ann. But what does that *mean?*" (p. 134).

Sad to say, Myra has also acquired Robbe-Grillet's passion for italicizing key words.

In the opening pages of *Myra*, Vidal has made clear to those who have read Sartre and Robbe-Grillet (that blessed minority) exactly what he is doing. The novel is a joke, a literary and even an academic one. The recording of banality has become the apotheosis of banality, a characteristic of both the New Novel and the films of the forties. Myra knows she can never define her nature since nothing is what it seems to be. But she can copulate with herself, for what is a diary other than the *moi* penetrating the *soi* in an act of perfect narcissism?

Myra is also a parody of literature, showing the nadir to which art can plunge when it abandons its canons. Since Myra believes that the only valid form of literature today is the memoir, she can achieve the absolute truth she craves through a diary that is continually tending toward cinema. Unlike the novel, the film exists only in the present tense. If words have become too wounded to convey reality, then celluloid, "*blessed* celluloid," can heal them by minimizing their importance, converting the verbal into the visual, and unfolding "the absolute truth, copied precisely from life, preferably at the moment it is happening" (p. 18).

The displacement of the written word by the visual media is one of Vidal's recurring fears. To show how such a displacement can happen, he has constructed a plot that explodes the very nature of plot, reducing it to the level of dream, where the heart of film resides.

Myra, allegedly the widow of film critic Myron Breckinridge, arrives in Los Angeles to claim her inheritance from her "husband's" uncle, onetime cowboy star Buck Loner. The estate, formerly an orange grove, has been converted into the profitable Academy of Drama and Modeling. Buck is suspicious of the wily Myra but offers her a position teaching posture and empathy. Although Myra becomes the Academy's star teacher, she still broods about Myron's failure to become a major critic. Furthermore, she bears a personal grudge against the American male for his virility and embarks upon a campaign to avenge her husband's death (suicide?) by emasculating whomever she can.

Myra has to look no further than Rusty Godowsky, who, in addition to being a stud, also has poor posture. On her first attempt to debase him, she gives him a routine examination for scoliosis during which she is nearly transported with ecstasy when she discovers he wears Jockey shorts. Learning that Rusty never took the required physical, she summons him to the infirmary where she subjects him to a pre-induction agony—urine specimen, hernia examination, and syphilis test—interspersed with indelicate questions about his sex life with Mary-Ann Pringle. The naïve Rusty misconstrues the physical as a bizarre prelude to sex with Myra, who thereupon straps him to the examining table and rapes him with a dildo.

At this point, the novel veers off into comedy that is neither dark nor crepuscular but downright malevolent. Entry 29 has produced queasiness in the strongest of stomachs, yet one might ask if the Rape of Rusty (a phrase so academically alliterative that it conjures up the Death of Dido) is quite so depraved as it seems. The episode was transferred with much mutilation to the film, where it depressed director Michael Sarne to such an extent that he winced when he discussed it on a talk show. While the former pop singer turned *auteur* deplored a novel that depicted, as he called it, "the rape of a young boy," he managed to subdue his rage long enough to direct the film version. He even translated the equine image of Myra mounting Rusty like a bronco buster to a "Ride 'em, cowboy!" shot of Raquel Welch doing everything but crying "Hi-Yo, Silver, Awa-a-ay!" while straddling Roger Herren's buttocks.

How revolted should one feel? We have come a long way since 1968 when *Myra* hit the bookstores with virtually no fanfare. We have had, and have been had by, *Oh! Calcutta!*, nude ballet, a well-hung Jesus and Moses in *Lenny*, a Christus figure emptying his bladder on the cross in Arrabal's *And They Put Handcuffs on the Flowers*. How innocent Myra was, compared to such sophisticates!

Unfortunately, any academic seeking to discuss *Myra* critically must justify his attempt by citing the work of another academic. I shall therefore cite Purvis E. Boyette's epochal "*Myra Breckinridge* and Imitative Form" (*Modern Fiction Studies*, Summer 1971). To use the time-honored professorial cliché, "I quote": "Myra's seduction of Rusty Godowsky is the narrative climax of the book; it is also the satirical center. The question for any serious reader is whether this act of perversion is artistically valid" (p. 235).

Perhaps one should try to be scholarly for a moment and placate those outraged souls who swooned when Myra strapped down a youth in the bloom of manhood and rammed her dildo against his petaled sphincter (note the floral imagery). It will probably make no difference to them if one insists that: (1) Rusty is no more real than Myra; (2) His rape is symbolic; (3) Even if it is taken literally, Rusty does not rebel during the ordeal and, however dazed, leaves Myra with a " 'Thank you, ma'am' "; and (4) He later becomes a homosexual, courtesy of the omniscient Myra who simply put the Socratic philosophy, "Know thyself," into practice.

Classroom criticism delights in the establishment of motives. Tripartite motivation is best, since "three," apart from being a mystical number, admits of gradation or, as rhetoricians used to say, "ascending order." While Myra has three reasons for her nefarious deed, they do not constitute a hierarchy but remain interrelated. She wishes to destroy Rusty's bourgeois notion of masculinity, to avenge Myron, who submitted to anal penetration, and to prevent a superstud from breeding indiscriminately. Thus she becomes the handmaiden of the Mother Goddess, the heroic vindicator, and the patriotic Malthusian—all subsumed under one blazing title: The Awesome Amazon, whose exploits are unfolded in installments like the chapters in a serial.

Professor Boyette is correct in calling the Rape of Rusty "the narrative climax" of the novel, but there is the dénouement to consider. An automobile accident leaves Myra breastless and bearded. The moment of truth has come; Myra, *né* Myron Breckinridge, is a transsexual. However, her reversal to masculine form, if not to masculinity itself, has certain redeeming features which will satisfy the moralist and fantasist alike. The restored Myron can wed Mary-Ann, who must resign herself to a childless marriage; and after an attempt to conquer Hollywood, restore matriarchy, and make the daylight dream a twenty-four-hour reality, Myron/ Myra realizes that "happiness, like the proverbial bluebird, is to be found in your own backyard if you just know where to look."

It may surprise the porno people to learn that *Myra* can be read on several levels. One could take the novel as the tale of a transsexual or the wish-fulfillment of every homoerotic who yearned to destroy his masculinity and emerge from the severed scrotum as the New Aphrodite, hell-bent on emasculation. Fans of *Wonder Woman* comics would see Myra as the apotheosis of their favorite Amazon princess from Paradise Isle. Like Vidal's novel, the comic book always began with a manifesto of feminine superiority. Myra announces at the outset how she held off the Trobriand Islanders with a stone ax which she used to break the balls of their finest warriors. Wonder Woman never broke balls (although she would have been quite proficient at it); but she did claim the power to burst the fetters of evil, deflect bullets with her steel bracelets, and bring enemies to their knees with her golden magic lasso.

If one can make the assumption that the transsexual operation is a metaphor for androgyny, then another interpretation is possible. When the feminine principle predominates in Vidal's androgyne, her name will be Myra and she will seduce a male—Rusty. But when the masculine principle overwhelms the feminine, his name is Myron and he gravitates toward a female—Mary-Ann. Yet this is not entirely accurate, for Myra, even when she is Myra, can be sexually attracted to Mary-Ann; and when the androgyne was Myron, the film critic, he was an easily buggered fag. Myra even transcends the mythical androgyne and becomes the amalgamation of every sexual type: male/heterosexual, female/heterosexual, male/homosexual, female/lesbian—in short, ultimate sexuality.

One might conceive of Myra as a self-evolving, self-transforming phenomenon; or in Anaximander's terms, a primal mass in perpetual motion, a whirling nebula releasing each of the sexes that was originally locked within it. A fantastic theory, of course; but no more fantastic than Anaximander's cosmogony. Myra/Myron is the sexual apeiron, and as such has no boundaries unless the author imposes them by way of a plot. As heterosexual female, *she* can seduce a male; as heterosexual male, *he* can marry a female; as lesbian, *she* can caress a girl's breasts; as homosexual, *he* can be sodomized, much to his discomfort. If, as Bette Davis claimed in her autobiography *The Lonely Life* (1962), sex is "God's joke on humanity," then *Myra Breckinridge* is humanity's reply.

Vidal has despaired of anyone's understanding *Myra* without the aid of the Classics, particularly Plato's *Symposium* and Petronius' *Satyricon*. In the *Symposium*, the playwright Aristophanes explains the origin of the sexes in a wildly imaginative myth. Originally there were three sexes—male, female, and a third we now derogatorily call androgynous. The sexes were spherical in shape because their progenitors were spherical; males sprang from the sun, females from the earth, and androgynes from the double-sexed moon. In happier days, the sexes possessed twice the number of appendages, including genitalia, that they do now. But, alas, the sexes were rebellious, and Zeus decided to cleave them in two. Consequently, halves of the androgyne developed into heterosexuals; halves of the female became lesbians; and halves of the males, homosexuals. So it is that each of us is doomed to search for our other half in an effort to regain that pre-lapsarian unity.

Isn't Myra pursuing the same goal—that mythical oneness that existed before the fall? Her aim, to destroy any vestigial remains of manhood, no doubt makes her a freak to some; yet behind *Myra Breckinridge* with its (horrifying) "rape of a young boy," there is an almost simple-minded innocence. One cannot even take Rusty's debasement seriously; as Vidal describes it, it is more of a last roundup or the fleecing of a lamb that does not chafe under the shears. In terms of the *Symposium* myth,

Rusty, the half of the Ur-Male, naturally becomes a homosexual—what else? But what of poor Myra? Since she is (or was) the original androgyne, she would have had, in a happier incarnation, four sex organs which could admit of various forms of ingress.

Myra's tragedy was her attempt to live the role of the original androgyne; and halved androgynes, according to the myth, are doomed to heterosexuality, which is her ultimate fate. It is strange that the more civilized we are, the more we claim to be androgynous; yet our acts belie our claim, and we literally settle for half. Such was Myra's destiny, and such is the destiny of all who stem from what Plato calls "that composite sex." Myra can only playact at being the nebula from which the sexes separate as it whirls through space; sometimes she separates with them, enclosing herself in whatever gender happens to be splitting off. A transsexual operation only defers the day of reckoning; once a male, always a male, and never the twain shall meet.

The tragic persona can be seen as an exaggeration of the comic. Tragedy and comedy are often interrelated; the Chaplinesque clown is King Lear in whiteface and baggy pants. *Myra Breckinridge* masquerades as comic art, yet if analyzed closely, it ends in tragedy. Myra never founds the matriarchy of her dreams, nor does she eradicate the vestigial remains of Rusty's manhood: she merely exposes his true nature. Even more disconcerting is her failure to complete her study of Parker Tyler. Her operation was a fiasco, and she never received her share of the property. All Myra acquired for her misspent efforts was a spouse who never heard of the Andrews Sisters and the bluebird of happiness chirping away in the backyard of their San Fernando Valley home. The latter, it would seem, makes up for everything.

Vidal has often forced a happy ending from material that was intractably tragic. But the films of the forties also painted the gray clouds with sunshine. The B-Western often portrayed a plucky heroine arriving at a frontier town to claim the homestead bequeathed to her in Daddy's will. She is all *animus*—totally self-sufficient and scornful of offers of protection. The villains lay their snares, which almost enmesh her, but invariably a lonesome cowboy comes to the heroine's aid, and in the course of the film it is he, not she, who guns down the culprits, restores the proerty, and in the fade-out is sharing it with her.

The heroine has failed; she simply couldn't do it single-handedly. Moreover, the estate is no longer "hers" but "theirs." But to the average moviegoer, the heroine has scored a triumph, for in the final long shot she and her lover survey their domain as the setting sun slowly dissolves into THE END. The film succeeds where the heroine did not; the resolution actually negates her original intention. Yet in film ethics, love is never a negation; it is merely the substitution of one goal for another. Marriage replaces rugged individualism, and the exchange is made so imperceptibly that one never notices the heroine traded gold for brass.

So it was with Myra Breckinridge. She failed in her endeavors, but won a mate and a bluebird. She was victim and victor, but in the vocabulary of dream, they are synonymous.

From the early sixties on, Gore Vidal has claimed he is a literary descendant of Petronius, the wit of the Neronian Age whose *Satyricon* formed the basis of Fellini's most self-indulgent film. It is a claim that was reinforced by Gerald Clarke's "Petronius Americanus" (*The Atlantic*, March 1972), where Vidal emerged as "the Petronius of the last days of the American empire." Petronius occupies a strange position in the Academy. Latin teachers, depressed by declining enrollments, would slyly encourage their wards to become fluent enough in the language so they could read the untranslatable passages of the *Satyricon* in the original—a goal to which only a few could aspire. Yet when one does read the novel, even in William Arrowsmith's translation,[5] it seems peculiarly tame and soberly moralistic. Moreover, only a fraction survives of what may have been a twenty-book work.

Petronius' novel is a parody—not a lampoon or a travesty but something "subtly rooted in admiration," to use William Golding's definition. The *Satyricon* is a parody of the *Odyssey* in this specialized sense of the word; it may strike the novice as the willful desecration of an idol, unless he realizes it is a tribute to something which is indisputably great but which, because times and circumstances change, can never return as it was. Perhaps it would be better to call the *Satyricon* an anti-*Odyssey*, without the negativism the prefix implies. It is an *envoi* to the glory that was Greece and an ambiguous salutation to the decadence that is Imperial Rome.

The *Satyricon* is also a dream-narrative about a picaresque trio whose exploits defy verisimilitude in a way that Odysseus' did not. It reflects a world where objects regain the terrifying significance they had before man reduced their power and where benevolent humans become folkloric ogres issuing from the collective unconscious like a congress of demons that disappears when the dreamer awakens. But the dreamer need feel no inadequacies; in the *Satyricon*, the heroic is geared to everyone's level.

What we possess of the *Satyricon* is a narrator's account of his exploits—an account that does not obey any empirico-literary laws but rather the shifting mandates of the folk tale. The narrator is Encolpius ("The Crotch"), and his companions are Ascyltus ("The Unmolested") and Giton ("Neighbor"). Encolpius is an educated decadent; he knows his Roman rhetoric well enough to lament the decline of old-fashioned Ciceronian eloquence:

> . . . it was you rhetoricians who more than anyone else strangled true eloquence. By reducing everything to sound, you concocted this bloated puffpaste of pretty drivel whose only real purpose is the pleasure of punning and the thrill of ambiguity. Result? Language lost its sinew, its nerve. Eloquence died. (pp. 21–22)

Myra was familiar enough with the standards of fiction to know that they all but collapsed in the sixties:

> The novel being dead, there is no point to writing made-up stories. Look at the French who will not and the Americans who cannot. (p. 4)

Myra stoically accepts what Encolpius bemoans—the death of language and the end of traditional art.

To Petronius, the Golden Age had passed; in its absence, he created a pastiche where prose branches off into poetry, and styles weave in and out of each other. Like most novelists wrongly accused of being pornographers, Petronius was quite conservative and believed in simplicity of language. To illustrate the polyglot of his age, he wrote a satire in the root meaning of the word—

a mélange where the classical melts into the baroque, the sublime into the vulgar, and prose narrative into poetic *divertissement.*

Myra is also a pastiche. The cool, precise language of the diary alternates with the "Buck Loner Reports" on recording discs. While Myra knows how to round out a sentence, quote accurately (if not in context), and italicize film titles, Buck Loner can only entrust his disconnected thoughts to a machine that reproduces their ungrammatical and asyntactical barbarisms:

... that doctor friend of hers will swear he was a witness which is what it sounded like on the long distance telephone call that was bugged and what do we do then I ask you question mark ... (p. 150)

Another feature the *Satyricon* shares with *Myra* is the use of the *porte-parole*, where the characters become the author's spokesmen. Petronius has put some of his deepest convictions into the mouths of sodomites and pederasts. Encolpius the Crotch, an educated bisexual and a murderer, inveighs against the education of his day and the decline of literary values; later, Eumolpus, a poet-pederast, takes up the refrain:

As for our own times, why, we are so besotted with drink, so steeped in debauchery, that we lack the strength even to study the great achievements of the past. One and all, we traduce the dead and slander our great tradition. ... What, I ask you, has become of logic and dialectic? (p. 93)

Myra, the transsexual sodomizer, summarizes in her diary what her creator has expounded in his essays and interviews:

After some three hundred years the novel in English has lost the general reader . . . and I propose that he will not again recover his old enthusiasm.
—"A Note on the Novel" (1956)

We may now be on the verge of having a civilization—small, but all our own—but it looks like it may not be interested in novels.
—"Disturber of the Peace: Gore Vidal" (1961)

To say that no one now much likes novels is to exaggerate very little. The large public which used to find pleasure in prose fiction prefers movies, television, journalism and books of fact.
—"French Letters: Theories of the New Novel" (1967)

It has been observed that American men do not read novels because they feel guilty when they read books which do not have facts in them. Made-up stories are for women and children; facts are for men.
—"Writers and the World" (1967)

The novel being dead, there is no point to writing made-up stories.
—*Myra Breckinridge* (1968)

Structurally, if one can even use the phrase, the *Satyricon* has an engaging looseness and, like *Myra*, an order within that looseness. It is a dream-narrative where characters disappear only to return without a plausible explanation and where friendships dissolve only to mend miraculously. The *Satyricon* opens with a disquisition on literature which ends abruptly as the narrator attempts to locate his lodgings. A mysterious crone beckons and leads him to a brothel where he discovers Ascyltus. A quarrel over Giton's favors almost brings about the parting of the ways, but an adventure in the form of the recovery of a stolen tunic temporarily restores their tenuous camaraderie. The picaros no sooner recover their treasure when they wander into an orgy where slaves turn into thieves and eunuchs become anal-erotics. One phantasmagoria leads to another; the orgy at Quartilla's is followed by the banquet at Trimalchio's that is no less nightmarish.

The second half of the novel duplicates the form of the first, beginning as it does on a literary note (a poet's attack on degenerate art) and then moving from the ordered to the chaotic. With the departure of Ascyltus, one of those dispensable characters of fairy tale (easily introduced and easily written out), a new trio emerges: Encolpius, Giton, and Eumolpus.

The dream does not tolerate the encroachments of form; the union of characters suggests the imposition of order with which fantasy is always warring. Encolpius, Giton, and Eumolpus board a ship, only to discover its owner is Lichas, an old enemy. At the critical moment, a tempest dispenses with Lichas, and the trio finds itself in Crotona where Encolpius, like Myra, becomes a legacy-hunter—as common a sport in the cinema (con-women, card sharpers, gold diggers) as it was in Imperial Rome.

Like a whirlpool, the dream-narrative draws its characters into a vortex, cycling them through a mad world where sodomites extol classical art and the *nouveaux riches* pervert it. Encolpius enters the whirlpool a Neronian beat and comes forth a legacy-hunter with a new name, Polyaenus; The Crotch has become The Much-Praised, one of Odysseus' epithets. Unfortunately, he has also been changed from Encolpius the Potent to Polyaenus the Impotent, a highly undesirable title for one who intends to live off rich women. But one day, *mirabile dictu*, Encolpius opens his tunic and discovers a bobbing erection. Like Myra, he has been disenchanted; his potency was restored as miraculously as Myra's gender (if not her sex).

In both the *Satyricon* and *Myra*, transformation is the stage prior to the happy ending. How the *Satyricon* ended one will never know; the text breaks off with the perverse Eumolpus making a will requiring his beneficiaries to dismember his body and devour the pieces before the entire city. But if Petronius' novel is an anti-*Odyssey* as well as a dream-narrative, it should end like the epic and the dream—with the resolution of antinomies; and if Arrowsmith's conjecture is correct, with the union of a bisexual Odysseus figure with his Penelope. For only in a dream could Encolpius make it with a heroine of legend; and only in a dream could *Myron redivivus* wed Mary-Ann Pringle.

I have argued earlier that Myra was an innocent bred in those houses of illusion that once were called movie theatres. Yet Professor Boyette, who is careful to observe that "Vidal is obviously everything that Myra is not" (a truism if there ever was one), regards Myra herself as a symbol of "American culture, ahistorical, empty of traditional values, and artistically shallow" (p. 235). One could say the same about the world of Petronius and reach the conclusion that Imperial Rome and modern America produce glamorous vulgarians—another link in the chain of comparisons for those who see no difference between the Fall of the Roman Empire and the Decline of the American Republic.

Myra is not Petronius' Trimalchio, the ex-slave turned *nouveau riche*, who confuses the little knowledge he has and dates Hannibal at the time of the Trojan War, assigns matricide to Cassandra, and recalls a bas-relief of Daedalus locking up Niobe in the Trojan Horse. Myra's knowledge may be limited and academically of little consequence, but it is accurate. She may only know "books about books," but that is no mean achievement in an age when audiences base their opinion of a novel they never read on the film version they just saw. And if she is "ahistorical, empty of traditional values," it is because she spends too much time breaking the code of the films of the forties to find their hidden meaning, and not enough time searching for ambivalence in serious literature. Literary ambivalence would elude Myra; one can hardly believe she would understand or even care about it. Yet the films Myra cherishes had their peculiar ambivalence—not the conscious sort one finds in works like *Death in Venice,* but the imposed kind that came from the Breen Office, which required "the other level" to exist in the sphere of innuendo or in that limbo between a kiss by the blazing fireplace and the quiescence that follows the last of the embers.

In setting the films of the forties alongside the achievements of Shakespeare and Michelangelo, and calling Parker Tyler "the central thinker of our age," Myra is no worse than any star-worshiper of her generation. Her hope for another masterpiece like that wartime tearjerker *Since You Went Away* (1944) is understandable because one hears the same plea today from the addicts of the past who recoil from the reality of contemporary cinema and melt away with the snows of yesteryear. Myra mocks the New Novel, which is nothing more than a disguised scenario with the camera eye replacing the teller of the tale. The New Novel *is* film, translating words into shots and paragraphs into sequences; but Myra cannot accept either the New Novel or the new cinema because they negate *her* concept of film, which is simply a crossword puzzle where the contestant supplies his own key.

Myra, then, is as ambivalent as her favorite era. When she chooses, she can speak eloquently about the demise of the novel and the birth of the Neanderthal tube-watchers. But in trying to achieve the genderless sexuality of the films of the forties, she falls victim to the Hollywood commonplace that there are as many sexes in a given film as there are characters. In the movies, particularly in those of the forties where stars were carefully selected to illustrate certain sexual types, there were no such entities as "male" and "female." There were male *types* and female *types*; one never thought of a male per se, but rather of a "Cary Grant" male or a "Gary Cooper" male. Each actor projected his own brand of masculinity, but never total manhood. The girl-shy cowboy, the gangster who degraded his moll, the debonair man about town who selected his clothes and his women with equal fastidiousness, the orphan boy who joined the cattle drive to find a father-surrogate: all of these types became separate sexes on the screen, totally free of the limitations that gender places on humans.

Sex without gender was the inevitable by-product of the star system, which offered endless alternatives to the male-female, either-or dichotomy of nature. There has never been so much sexual diversity on the screen as there was in the forties; nor has there ever been so much myth.

As a creature of myth, Myra requires its sustenance

against reality. But she can not find it in the sixties, which severely reduced the number of possibilities within the once-unlimited categories of Male and Female. Consequently, she begins to take the television commercial seriously because it showed signs of replacing the other visual arts. Small wonder, for the commercial is the last stronghold of myth, or rather myth in its uncritical stage. It illustrates all the characteristics of the dream-narrative and its lowest literary form, the fairy tale: irresponsibility, the gratification of desires, the encouragement of wishful thinking, the happy ending, and the triumph of the unfortunate person. The commercial fulfills one's wildest dreams, with detergents that turn clothes immaculate without polluting the rivers, cleansing agents that transform floors into mirrors, setting lotions that produce beauty parlor coiffures. Ugly ducklings triumph through mouthwashes and deodorant sprays, toothpaste and talcum.

The commercial also depicts the entire range of *Märchen*—talking animals (Charlie the Tuna, Morris the Cat); Promethean culture heroes rowing their boats in toilet tanks or dispensing plastic bags for hygienic householders; Hermes figures like Josephine the Plumber; and the Olympians themselves (the Imperial Margarine users with their crowned heads). MYRA LIVES! And she will continue to live as long as there are those who wonder whether the fastidious cats that only eat Nine Lives are furry closet queens or whether the airline stewardesses who purr "Fly me" are really asking to be laid.

"We are, I know not how, double in ourselves, so that what we believe we disbelieve, and cannot rid ourselves of what we condemn," wrote Montaigne. To close debate as to whether Myra is the American monster or the American innocent, let us say that neither she nor her creator can rid themselves of what they condemn. For years Vidal has been experiencing a love-hate relationship with television and the movies, although he wrote for both media with some success. He scorns the non-novel, yet he wrote a superb one—*Two Sisters: A Memoir in the Form of a Novel.* He loves to relate how he went into a paroxysm of laughter in a Los Angeles hotel when he turned on the television and heard Bette Davis telling Paul Henreid in *Now Voyager* to stop looking for the moon when they had the stars.

For a man of letters, Gore Vidal is uncomfortably knowledgeable about the films of the forties. Once I asked whether Myra's name was suggested by a character called Mary Breckinridge in *The Sailor Takes a Wife.* He replied with his usual world-weariness: "*The Sailor Takes a Wife* . . . MGM . . . 1945 . . . June Allyson, Robert Walker, Audrey Totter." Then he paused: "No. Her name was suggested by a female impersonator."

$\curvearrowright$ 10

The Hieroglyphs of Time

AS A PRIVATE PERSON, Vidal despises the curious; he has been known to seat inquisitorial interviewers in a draft and to accompany journalists seeking definitive proof of his sex life to a bar where he would promptly leave them in their cups and stroll off with a hooker. As a novelist, he knew his career was too well publicized for masquerade; he was therefore continually searching for a form that could allow him to reveal what he wanted to without making a total disclosure. In an effort to unite his life with his work before both passed into the embalming prose of biography, Vidal experimented with depersonalized heroes, transparent names, a tentative parallelism between author and character, and false clues to trap the sleuth in his own guessing game.

The search for the perfect form was complicated by

Vidal's desire to be an essayist as well as a writer of fiction. While the essayist bemoaned the death of fiction, the novelist continued to produce it. *Myra Breckinridge* was an attempt to conciliate the warring halves of a divided self through a work that was neither an essay nor a novel, but a diary where the conscious mind explored its unconscious state. With *Myra*, Vidal abandoned the conventional novel for a diary of the psyche where "I/ Myra" became the ultimate *"Madame Bovary, c'est moi."*

Myra reduced the critical commonplace of an author's becoming one with his characters to the absurdity of self-copulation; but *Two Sisters* (1970), aptly subtitled *A Memoir in the Form of a Novel*, argued even more forcefully that an author impregnates not only himself but also everything impinging upon his senses. *Two Sisters* resides at the crossroads of art where characters—imaginary, disguised, and real—interact; where the novelist debates with his critical alter ego; and where a novel, a scenario, a memoir, and a journal cross-fertilize each other. At the end, one must wonder, as indeed the author did, which of the four creations is the most truthful. It is not even a matter of believing the tale (in this case four of them) or the teller; does one believe the novel, the film script, the narrator's recollection of the past, or the journal's quite different reconstruction? "What is truth?" as Pontius Pilate asked Jesus Christ, who significantly refused to answer.

The novel or the fictional narrative (or is it fictional at all?) can easily be disentangled from the journal and the scenario. In 1968, the narrator (later identified as V.) is in Rome with an old flame, Marietta Donegal, mistress of everyone who was anyone and specialist in the art of "flowing." The former lovers delight in challenging each other's interpretations of the past. Marietta has discovered her own way of preserving her memories; she dips them in the Waters of Oblivion until they acquire the appearance of washed-out pastels and are ready for publication. Having published five volumes of memoirs in an "ensorcelling" style (a word she admires for its semantic exoticism), Marietta attempts to cajole the narrator into writing a critique of her work with the same feeling he lavished on *The City and the Pillar*.

A clue at last! To anticipate the questions of posterity, *le narrateur, c'est lui;* and make of it what you will—a true confession, a confession of truth, or their conversion into fiction that purges truth of its candor, confession of its conscience.

Vidal has admitted (hosanna!) . . . but admitted *what?* That he was born under Libra and once had an affair with a diarist? The narrator's references to *The City and the Pillar* and to Nabokov's tirade in *Time* against *Myra Breckinridge* can easily seduce the reader into believing the novel will unwind the mummy wrappings in a neat coil and reveal the author in his ancient nakedness: enter Vidal nude and maimed, Petronius' *Satyricon* and Gide's *Notebooks of André Walter* under each stump-like arm. Vidal will admit much more in *Two Sisters*, but the admissions are encased in a book that is constantly vacillating between past and present, each of which has its own subdivisions—past/present as truth, past/present as fiction.

The novel that began with two ex-lovers reconstructing the past turned into a memoir with Marietta's disclosure of Eric Van Damm's death. Eric, a promising (or was he?) film maker and one of Marietta's former bedmates, died while photographing (not really) a Berkeley riot; among his possessions were a journal and an unfilmed scenario. The narrator knew Eric and his twin sister, Erika—the present incarnations of Myron and Myra. Erika was dark, and Eric fair; like the twins in John Horne Burns' *A Cry of Children* (1952) who are described as "two yolks in the same egg," Eric and Erika represent the halved anima. Naturally a narrator, similarly divided, would be attracted to a pair of *Wunderkinder*, selecting Erika as a sometime mistress and Eric as a boy-companion. Again Fiedler's *Love and Death in the American Novel* elucidates V.'s attraction to twins: ". . . the mirror-image of the self is translated in the American novel either into the flesh of one's flesh, the sister as *anima;* or into the comrade of one's own sex, the buddy as *anima*" (p. 348).

When the narrator begins reading the journal, he discovers another Eric and another self. To Eric, the narrator was merely V., a young American magus roaming about Paris in the summer of 1948, dispensing ideas about art and sex like pep pills for the creatively lethargic, arguing *ad nauseam* with Tennessee Williams about violence in the theatre, and turning prickly when anyone spoke of *The City and the Pillar* without reverence.

V. reacts to the journal the same way one would respond to hearing a familiar tape edited or played in reverse. The questions that plague him as he reads incredulously about himself, his friend, and the sister they shared would be answerable only if some transcript of the summer of 1948 were extant; since none is, V. must resurrect the period from time's oubliette—a period he recalls differently from Eric.

V. has no recollection of the scenario *The Two Widows of Ephesus*, which Eric claimed he read. The script was one of those bloated classical epics that, had it been filmed in 1948, could never have starred Ava Gardner and Lana Turner as the producer planned, but probably Maria Montez, in all her lacquered regality, playing a dual role à la *Cobra Woman* (1943). For the two sisters in *The Two Widows of Ephesus* were really profiles of the same Janus face, no more believable as siblings than Eric and Erika were.

For the moment, one should accept the noble lie of fiction and regard the ladies in the scenario as sisters. Helena is the widow of the Great King of Persia; but the title is too cumbersome for the masses, so she will be known as the late Emperor's wife or simply as the Empress. Artemisa, the older sister, is the wife of a demoted Carian satrap; but since satraps (or Caria for that matter) are intelligible only to those who read Xenophon or Herodotus, the script reduces her complicated status to Queen. Technically, neither sister is an Empress nor a Queen; historically, they are improbabilities; dramatically, they are bores. But no matter. They are the offspring of a royal family headed by Lagus, an Ephesian patrician, and Arsinoë, who "launched and lost her famous daughters."

Thus far the script is no more complex than any "sand and sex" epic; based on the premise that intricacy of plot compensates for paucity of thought, it dupes the moviegoer into believing he has witnessed something profound when he has only meandered through genealogy.

Helena's plight is even more poignant than that of the average widowed Empress; she has a three-year-old son who must have his chance at the throne, preferably when he is older. Moreover, although hers was "the greatest marriage of all time," it was not particularly monogamous; Helena was only one of a harem that included her husband's own daughter.

Meanwhile Artemisa, the childless sister, has been having an affair with Achoris, a slave's son, a Greek, a yachtsman, and (coincidentally) the richest man in the world. Achoris came to Ephesus to woo Helena, who enthralled him when he first saw her "palely reflected in her sister's eyes"—another clue that one sister was merely the mote in the other's eye. Helena, pregnant with her half-brother's child, accepts the proposal, which is made more attractive by the prospect of permanent residence on a yacht. And if a floating home is not enough, Achoris promises her a floating island.

When Artemisa's husband dies of a fever, widowhood gives the two sisters a common bond. Their reunion is only temporary, for Artemisa suddenly announces *her* marriage to Achoris and encourages Helena to bear the nuptials with resignation. At that moment, Herostratus decides to usurp the spotlight from the two sisters by burning the Temple of Diana. He is last seen in a prison cell, where he relates the story, arguing that a rebel who burned a wonder of the world far surpasses two sisters in love with a Greek potentate; and that he, not his half-sisters, is the real star of the show.

The original scenario was not even Eric's; he was only asked to adapt it for the screen. But in the adaptation, he defied the censors and transferred his own incest with Erika to his characters, thereby creating a parallelism between Eric/Erika and Helena/Herostratus. The scenario is one ring revolving within a concentric pattern where mechanical time encircles time remembered; it is also the microcosm of the novel, which is largely V.'s attempt to determine whether life is the orbit of fiction or fiction the orbit of life.

In a bizarre way, the script was a malevolent prophecy where the characters Eric thought were fictitious became their living counterparts and wrote their own plot which sometimes ran parallel to, but often deviated from, the original. *The Two Widows of Ephesus*, like the novel in which it is enclosed, complements/negates the present, prophesies/contradicts the future, reflects/reworks the past.

Erika Van Damm conceived her brother's child just as Helena conceived Herostratus'; but Erika found a rich husband just in time, while Helena lost Achoris to her sister. By identifying with Herostratus' mania for immortality, Eric threw himself into a burning house. He never died the heroic death Marietta described in her memoir, for there was no film in his camera when he was photographing the Berkeley riot. Herostratus, however, did not die by setting afire the Temple of Diana. Eric allowed his character to live; but he himself chose to undergo the fate Herostratus would have suffered if justice had prevailed.

In 1948, Eric Van Damm could only have conceived of two sisters like Helena and Artemisa as twin Madonnas in a perverse Holy Family. Little did he realize that almost twenty years later, Gore Vidal would write of another Holy Family, the Kennedys. In his famous but slightly dated 1967 essay,[1] Vidal argued that after the assassination, William Manchester, Arthur M. Schlesinger, Jr., Pierre Salinger, and a host of minor evangelists wrote the *Gospel of John Kennedy* as a passion play where an Osiris-Adonis-Christ figure was publicly murdered in the presence of eyewitnesses more numerous than those who attended the crucifixion on Calvary. The *Gospel*, promulgated as an article of faith, translated the life of the President into sacred history and converted his survivors into mythic deities; the widow became an Isis-Aphrodite-Madonna; and Bobby Kennedy, "Ares and perhaps Christ-to-be"—a short-lived honorific that seems, in retrospect, tragically prophetic.

The reviews of *Two Sisters* suggested the scenario concerned Vidal's "stepsister by marriage, Madame Aristotle Onassis." For the record, Gore Vidal's one-time stepfather, Hugh D. Auchincloss, was also Madame Onassis'; their bond of kinship is therefore tenuous, to say the least. The literary detective might enjoy unmasking the widowed Empress and the Greek potentate with his fabled yacht; yet he would only end up with an unstable equation where Achoris = Aristotle Onassis and Helena = Jacqueline Bouvier Kennedy—an equation that breaks down with Artemisa's marriage to Achoris.

Vidal is having the last laugh, challenging the voyeur to find the truth and then match it with Column A (Reality), Column B (Illusion), or Column C (Reality as Illusion). He had nothing to lose by being Pirandellian but his readers. The *Myra* aficionados knew *Two Sisters* would be double androgyny; and they alone could interpret Achoris' statement that he saw Helena in her sister's eye in terms of Ingmar Bergman's *Persona* (1966), where Elisabet and Alma are really halves of the same self.

Eric/Erika, Helena-Artemisa/Herostratus, for that matter, V./Marietta or even V./Eric, each of whom loved the prep school athlete who enlisted in the Marines and died in World War II. There is only one character in *Two Sisters:* the author playing a mirror game with his life.

In addition to being an elaborate metamorphosis of a novel into a memoir and a scenario, *Two Sisters* is a sexual fantasy where the dreamer begins by focusing on one image, which then multiplies itself into a hall of mirrors, each panel magnifying its erotic reflections. In such fantasies, there is always a hiatus between orgasms, an interim of quiescence when the dreamer turns from the imagined coupling of bodies to thoughts of the past. The other world of Eric's journal and his scenario summons V. back to 1948, which is lodged between the gates of horn and ivory, between truth and falsehood. Yet V. really cannot return to the past; he can only dream his way through it, reacting like Aeneas as he wandered among the shades. He cannot even read the journal or the script without stopping periodically to question, emend, or reconsider what Eric had written. Like the erotic dreamer, V. weaves in and out of bodies from the past, pausing for momentary lulls to reflect on more tangible memories like a dinner at Eleanor Roosevelt's cottage in Hyde Park, the eccentricities of Senator Gore, the founding of the New Party, and a tumble with Jack Kerouac in the Chelsea Hotel—all part of an intermission during coitus with *temps perdu.*

Had *Two Sisters* appeared in 1971, it would have been Vidal's anniversary novel celebrating a career that was then a quarter of a century old. As it happened, its publication in the summer of 1970 coincided with the release of the movie version of *Myra Breckinridge.* Vidal suspected the film would be a disaster; he also knew his name would be associated with it, although the final script was not his.

His suspicions were correct; the movie of *Myra* was universally despised, and one outraged critic dubbed

Twentieth-Century-Fox "Twentieth-Century-Skunk" for producing it. Never in the history of film criticism did so many reviewers express their wrath with such lack of wit. The stars managed to escape personal abuse because they were miscast (Raquel Welch), untalented (Rex Reed), or senescent (Mae West); but Vidal did not escape the slings and arrows that were flying from all quarters. During that summer when the air was heavy with morality, Gore Vidal, "the author of *Myra Breckinridge,*" was held responsible for a movie that offended everyone. It was odd that the critics who once distinguished between Dostoyevsky's *The Brothers Karamazov* and Richard Brooks' film of the same name could not separate Gore Vidal's *Myra Breckinridge* from Michael Sarne's.

Apparently nothing good could come from the pen of Gore Vidal. But the failure of *Two Sisters* was not entirely due to poor timing. The novel was foolishly advertised as a satire on Madame Onassis and Lee Radziwill; and the readers who expected to see Vidal wading triumphantly through a blood bath found him lounging in a frothy tub, languidly bursting the bubbles of the past.

On the eve, if not on the date, of his twenty-fifth year as a writer, Gore Vidal took a candid look at himself and his works as they moved in consort along the mirrored corridor of time. *Two Sisters* recalled *A Novel,* where the eighteen-year-old author struggled with conflicting points of view and finally offered the main character's autobiography as a partial corrective to the vagaries of human opinion; *The Judgment of Paris,* where the narrator's intrusive voice kept freezing the action into stills; *Messiah,* where an evangelist discovered himself through his own creation; and Myra's Petronian diary, which translated fiction into fantasy. *Two Sisters* seemed to be The Summing Up and perhaps even the Good-Bye to All That.

Yet it was not. In *Burr* (1973) he returned to the novel-memoir as an alternative to pure fiction or fictionalized biography, vindicating the American Catiline as he had vindicated the Apostate in *Julian* and himself in *Two Sisters*. One can understand why Vidal chose to cast *Burr* in a familiar mold. The novel-memoir had worked in the past. Historically, it was justifiable in view of Burr's own *Memoirs* and his *Private Journal,* both of which were edited by Matthew L. Davis, who also appears in the novel; artistically, it suited the author's twin talents. But Vidal had already broken the Heraclitean law by stepping twice into the same river. The waters of memory resist repeated attempts to part them, and perhaps Vidal played Moses once too often. While *Burr* is considerably more fascinating than *Two Sisters,* it does not achieve that unique mix of past and present where two years, 1948 and 1968, overlap like waves. In *Burr,* the present is always competing with the past, and fiction encroaching on fact; the result is an undeniably powerful, if disturbingly anarchic novel.

Fiction cannot be interwoven with history; it should be amalgamated with it. In *Burr,* the two go their separate ways, and one is forced to follow the autonomous path of each. The "fiction" within the novel concerns the attempt of Charlie Schuyler, a law clerk, to write a life of Colonel Burr. A simple request from William Leggett to compose a piece on Burr for the *Evening Post* turns Schuyler loose in the caverns of biography, where truth sneers at inference at every turn. Colorless reportage will not satisfy the radical Leggett, who is so committed to Jacksonian democracy that he will do anything to keep Martin Van Buren from becoming the eighth president of the United States. A pamphlet proving Van Buren is Burr's illegitimate son is his aim.

Thus begins the political education of Charlie Schuyler, who only wanted to make enough money as a writer to live abroad like James Fenimore Cooper. In true fairy tale fashion, Burr becomes the cooperative elf who gives Schuyler access to his notes on the Revolution. But Schuyler is an amateur biographer; overwhelmed by the complexity of his task, he describes everything ("I record it all"), sounding not unlike Myra in search of *le mot juste*. It is precisely in the fictional segment of *Burr* that one keeps hearing Myra's voice despairing of ever finding the perfect metaphor or the right tone. Should Schuyler call the green sunlight "infernal" or "subaqueous?" Does one speak of someone's "pursuit" or "place" of honor? Tenses change in mid-sentence, one word replaces another, and dashes erase half-formed thoughts.

Soon Burr begins dictating his Memoirs, and Schuyler becomes his faithful amanuensis as well as his surrogate son. However, he really was not playing son to the colonel. At the end of the novel, Schuyler, now an American consul living in Amalfi with an Italian wife, discovers he is one of Burr's illegitimate children.

The revelation is worthy of William Golding at his least inventive, although historically a case could be made for it. Charlie Schuyler is a shadowy kinsman of Charles Burdett, one of Burr's wards and perhaps his bastard son. Burdett, like the fictitious Schuyler, also worked in Burr's law office and was a writer of sorts, whose *Reminiscences of Aaron Burr, by One Who Knew and Loved Him*[2] was a touching account of the way Burr educated his protégés as if they were his natural children.

Burdett also fancied himself a novelist; he wrote in a quaint brownstone style that today could only be compared to a nightmare in which Louis Auchincloss dreamed he was Faith Baldwin. Vidal seems to have read some of Burdett's curiosities, especially *Margaret Moncrieffe* (also known as *The Beautiful Spy* and *Amours of Aaron Burr*) and *The Elliott Family; or, The Trials of New York Seamstresses*. *Margaret Moncrieffe* was a historical romance about the affair between Burr and the British spy who ended her days as a roving mistress. In the novel, Burr acknowledges the affair but corrects the impression that he and Margaret were legendary lovers: "I did not like the girl at all. Thought her precocious and sly." Burdett was also interested in the exploitation of seamstresses who fall prey to unprincipled employers. In the novel, Schuyler has a fling with a whore who turns out to be remarkably adept at making her own clothes.

Vidal's research is unassailable, yet one suspects the Schuyler/Burdett plot was designed to do more than provide a backdrop for the Memoirs which are at the heart of *Burr*. Reading the novel is rather like reading the actual *Memoirs of Aaron Burr*, which Matthew L. Davis edited by interleaving the correspondence with his own introductions and commentary. Through the double plot (The Adventures of Charlie Schuyler versus The Recollections of Aaron Burr), Vidal did convey something of the tension that exists between historical fact and its manifold interpretations. Perhaps he was also contrasting the preliminary research that goes into the writing of a biography (or the writing of *Burr*, for that matter) with the finished product; perhaps he was pitting the jottings of a hack against the lively prose of a master. *Tout comprendre c'est tout pardonner.* Whatever the reason, the fictional frame only bunches up the canvas it was designed to enclose.

The Memoirs scattered throughout the novel are another matter; quite simply, they represent the best writing Vidal has ever done. Schuyler may not have found the right tone, but Vidal has—a gentleman's tone, Madeira-smooth and so secure that it never grows hoarse from too many "seegars." By that peculiar interchange of creator and creation which few historical novelists can manage, Vidal becomes Burr, debunking his schoolbook image, giving a history lesson to Americans on the eve of their bicentennial, and dethroning the idols as swiftly as they were enshrined: the pock-marked Washington "who combined resolute courage with a total absence of imagination"; the bastard Hamilton who "never lied about issues, only men"; the Great Leveler Jefferson whose "insincerity is always spontaneous; it is never contrived."

In his political essays, Vidal's thesis has always been that rank does not give the Caesars imperial immunity, a position he allows Burr to adopt in his Memoirs. Indiscretions are divulged in the form of casual asides, as if the adulteries of Hamilton and Jefferson were too commonplace for a scholarly footnote. But when the charge of self-love which Washington leveled against Kennedy in *An Evening with Richard Nixon and . . .* is now directed at Washington, the purpose of the novel becomes clear. We are back in the world of *Washington, D.C.,* where Peter Sanford was contemplating a study of Burr and where Burden Day went to his death lamenting, "It has all gone wrong." What was this "it" without an antecedent? Apparently the America of yore, the Republic on paper.

In the past, Vidal merely inveighed against the republic turned empire; in *Burr,* he illustrated the transformation, suggesting it began when the Constitution was treated like an oracle that one praised if the prophecy was favorable or subverted if it was not. How American was Thomas Jefferson, who once championed the rights of the Western states to secede and then accused Burr of treason for allegedly trying to sever the Union at the Alleghenies? Even before the trial at Richmond, Jefferson declared Burr's guilt was "beyond question," sounding not unlike *princeps* Richard Nixon whose response to the Manson murders ("Here is a man who is guilty, directly or indirectly . . .") was similarly imprudent. How un-American was Aaron Burr, who fought a gentlemanly duel with Hamilton in 1804 and the following year was off to liberate Mexico and set himself up as its king? Vidal would argue that he was quintessentially American and that it was Jefferson who was the embryo Caesar.

The facts point to a man rather like Vidal himself, an aristocratic liberal whose ambitions for a political career were constantly frustrated. Having lost the presidential election of 1800 by a single vote in the House of Representatives, and then the governorship of New York, Burr had little choice but to begin the trek westward. His career in the East was over; there was a world elsewhere, and Burr, egged on by the double agent James Wilkinson, who finally betrayed him, was dreamer enough to think it conquerable.

Vidal is too scrupulous a historian to subscribe to the popular belief that Burr wanted to separate the West from the Union. Throughout his life, Burr denied this charge and in the novel he reduces the so-called right of secession to the absurd: ". . . no constitution can be effective if each state thinks that it has the right to nullify any federal law it pleases. I also think that as long as each state believes it has the right to secede, eventually one or more states *will* secede and there will be no United States."[3]

His main objective was the liberation of Mexico, where he naïvely believed the utopia that could never flourish on American soil could thrive with himself as philosopher-king:

But I can assure you that that early republic of ours was no place for a man who wanted to live in a good world, who wanted to make a true civilization and to share it with a host of choice spirits, such as I meant to establish in Mexico. Unfortunately, I was not able to be a king—though I very nearly was a president—but in my way I have been lucky for I have always been able to indulge my true passion which is to teach others, to take pleasure in bringing out the best in men and women, to make them *alive*, and though I did not achieve any sort of kingdom in this world, I have established small human dominions along my way . . . (p. 347)

Vidal was fortunate with *Julian;* the period was known only to a blessed minority that could appreciate the author's scholarship. But every American knows his history from textbooks, filmstrips, Carl Sandburg, or *1776;* and every American will measure *Burr* against his own conception or misconception of the Republic. Revisionists will applaud, Jeffersonians will seethe, and pedants who like their history neat will challenge the right of any novelist to invent when the facts are silent. No doubt some will cavil at Vidal's interpretation of the "despicable opinion" Hamilton expressed of Burr which led to the fatal duel. In the novel, Burr would never admit how despicable the opinion was, but Schuyler learned later that Hamilton had accused Burr of incest with his daughter Theodosia. Burr idolized Theo, and it is easy to see how a mind like Hamilton's that could not separate men from issues would be unable to distinguish between adulation and incest.

In *Burr*, Vidal is continuing the running debate with Jefferson that he began in "Homage to Daniel Shays" (1972), where he accused the Master of Monticello of being a Jekyll-Hyde demagogue. Vidal deplores the discrepancy between the Jefferson of the Declaration of Independence and the Jefferson of the Louisiana Purchase:

Subverting the Constitution he had helped create, Jefferson bought Louisiana from Napoleon, acquiring its citizens without their consent; he then proceeded to govern them as if they had been conquered, all the while secretly—comically—maneuvering, by hook or by crook, to bag the Floridas. The author of the Declaration of Independence was quite able to forget the unalienable rights of anyone whose property he thought should be joined to our empire—a word which crops up frequently in his correspondence.[4]

Apparently Massa Tom was the Caesar who transformed a potential empire into an actual one, although this is somewhat like blaming Pope Pius XII for the genocide of the Jews.

The America Vidal wants is a Platonic form that can survive transplantation without blemish. But even when one does return to the early days of the Republic (or the "empire *in posse*," as Vidal calls it), there was no unanimous opinion of what America should be; Federalists had one view, Republicans another. Nor do comparisons with Rome add much. The Roman constitution was pure *mos maiorum* and was never written down; the republic was an oligarchy, and the principate a monarchy. Fraudulence? Of course. How else could a city-state on the Tiber (or a polis on the Potomac) sustain an empire? The clearest enunciation of Rome's mission appears in literature, in Vergil's *Aeneid* to be precise, where Anchises tells his son that Rome's destiny is to "spare the conquered and strike down the haughty." Noble thoughts and worthy of the Mantuan. But literature is not life, and politics is not literature.

Burr leaves the reader in a state of helpless ambivalence. The idealist in us agrees with Burden Day: "It has all gone wrong." The pragmatist replies, "It could not have been otherwise." Finally, one is embarrassed at having to ponder the question the novel implicitly asks: "What *was* America?" Unfortunately, most of us can only reply in the present tense.

Postscript

IN THE LATE FORTIES, Gore Vidal was one of the most
promising of the postwar novelists; during the Golden
Age of Television, he was a leading script writer; when
live television was progressing toward immobility, he
turned to the scenario. After *Visit to a Small Planet*, he
was a Broadway satirist; with *The Best Man* he became a
political playwright. And if he is better known today as
an essayist than as a writer of fiction, it is because more
people read *The New York Review of Books* than the books
reviewed therein.

The novelist-critic is doomed to a double life, particularly in America, where the swinging pendulum never
rests. An age that is disenchanted with fiction gravitates
to journalism or to *New York* magazine, with its militant
antibelletrism and a style so slippery one slides through

the articles instead of reading them. What the cognoscenti admire about *New York* magazine is basically what the reviewers admire about Vidal: a frankness that is sometimes ballsy, rarely discreet, but never high-pitched.

The critics who extol Vidal's essays at the expense of his novels treat his prose as if it were some kind of pomade that makes the words glisten and the sentences stay in place. It is true that superficially—but only superficially—Vidal's occasional pieces are so well-groomed that they can easily be mistaken for slicked-down reportage. The language is nicely preened, but not fussy; tight, but not brittle; and it retains its aristocratic composure even when the author becomes earthy (*"God eats it, too!"*) and makes some carefully spaced admissions about getting the clap in Guatemala City or going to bed with a nymphomaniac.

Yet the rhetoric in the essays is light years removed from magazine ephemera. Vidal's love of gossip has deluded reviewers into thinking of him as a modern-day Suetonius. The appellation is fitting, but not for the reasons for which it was bestowed. Vidal and a few moribund classicists know that Suetonius, for all his anecdotes about the sexual propensities of the Caesars, wrote according to a strict format. Each of the *Lives* follows a systematic order: birth and family, early years, imperial acts, personal traits, last years and death. Suetonius worked his gossip into the *vita* form so that the reader who cared nothing about structure could giggle over the tidbits and the scholar who would ordinarily disregard sexual statistics could view them within the broader framework of the emperor's life.

Like Suetonius, Vidal tempers his gossip with art and

in a commercially devious way has also attracted a dual readership for his essays. However, one only hears from the first group—the reviewers who, in focusing merely on his wit, invective, and patrician disdain, have presented these qualities to the public as the stuff Vidal is made of. Yet a great essayist like Montaigne or Hazlitt will always find his personality in his subject and will convert what seems only topical and private into a universal statement. Vidal also possesses this art of translating the ephemeral into the timeless; it is an art that he learned from classical rhetoric.

Statement and proof, theme and *exempla:* these are the principles of writing from the trivium to Freshman Composition. What Vidal demands of a writer is clearly seen in "Doc Reuben," probably the best-known piece in the *Collected Essays.* Sex hucksters are easy prey for satirists; yet satirizing David Reuben, M.D., is like satirizing *Deep Throat,* a film that does not take itself seriously but at the same time asks the audience to accept its depiction of oral-genital sex as a joyous distraction from the boredom of straight screwing. Like *Deep Throat, Everything you always wanted to know about sex . . .* is neither vulnerable nor impregnable; as Myra in her Robbe-Grillet period would say, "It *is.* " Strike it and it remains defiantly stolid.

In "Doc Reuben," Vidal satisfies his obligations as a critic: he quotes a few passages, cracks some jokes, and in general satisfies the reader's curiosity about the book without revealing its total vacuity. But the piece is not about Doc Reuben; it is really an indictment of a supposed scientist's inability to prove his assertions that lesbianism is immature, that homosexual relationships are short-lived, and that Coca-Cola is an excellent douche. Vidal was so exasperated by Reuben's generalizations that he wrote "Prove?" ten times in the text. David Reuben is clearly ignorant of classical rhetoric, and Vidal will not allow his ignorance to go unchallenged. Statement and proof, theme and *exempla:* the hallmark of Vidal the essayist and one that must be stamped on any book he is asked to assess.

In "On Revising One's Work" (1965)[1] Vidal had to assess himself and convince the skeptics that a work of literature, once created, was not unalterable. A novice would have justified his revisions by citing the example of Henry James; of course, he also would have incurred the charge of hybris. Vidal was hardly a novice; instead of invoking the shade of James, he began by discussing one of James' short stories, "The Middle Years," in which an aging writer, an incurable perfectionist, reread his first novel and immediately started correcting the text. Vidal then mentioned, quite casually, that he had just revised *The City and the Pillar, The Judgment of Paris,* and *Messiah.* Before revealing the nature of the revisions, he advanced Cocteau's thesis that a work of art was never finished and Professor DuPee's belief that most of James' revisions were improvements. Slowly, he turned the essay into a defense of his own emendations, never allowing the "I" to become the sole pleader of the case but always tempering the opinions of the "I" with historical examples and strengthening them with an appeal to man's innate desire for self-improvement.

To anyone who respects symmetrical prose and subtle argumentation, Vidal's essays are nonpareil. Yet the essays exist in collections; while they are excerptable and eminently teachable as models of an all-but-abandoned-art, they do not add up to a full-scale work of nonfiction. But thus far Vidal has written thirteen novels—fourteen if one counts *The City and the Pillar Revised*—which he ranks over his essays. One need not accept the author's preference, but Vidal is sufficiently aware of the vagaries of literary history to know that while a writer can divine the public's taste, it never remains constant; and that the novelist-critic will eventually be judged by his fiction as soon as his essays are studied as rhetoric or reread for nostalgia.

Gore Vidal will always be known as a popular novelist, a term used disparagingly by the Academy, which often forgets that most of the novelists studied in literature courses were popular. Perhaps the day will come when the current mine of dissertation topics has been exhausted and doctoral students will be allowed to explore the way in which authors like Vidal, Updike, and Joyce Carol Oates, torn between writing commercially unsuccessful art novels and commercially successful pulp, salved their consciences by producing "popular art novels."

When it comes to fiction, Vidal is a classicist; his novels are as plot-centered as Aristotle would want them to be—traditional, often intricate, but rarely innovative. It is his classicism, not his expatriation or even his charmed life, that sets him apart from his contemporaries, most of whom discovered the sixties were ideal for breaking new ground in fiction because Vietnam had made literary standards almost as obsolescent as literature. The more eccentric a work was, the more profound it seemed to be. This was, after all, the era of the nonfiction novel (Capote's *In Cold Blood*), myth-mangling (Updike's *The Centaur*, Barth's *Giles Goat-Boy*), and the conversion of the American Dream into the American Nightmare (Mailer's *Why Are We in Vietnam?*).

While his colleagues were innovating, bleeding over

Vietnam, discovering entropy, and going with the flow, Vidal went about his business writing fiction with the proverbial beginning-middle-end, preferring to address himself to current affairs in his essays and quadrennial plays. Vidal the essayist faces the present, but Vidal the novelist looks to the past. The fact that *Why Are We in Vietnam?* (1967) appeared in the same year as *Washington, D.C.* not only crystallizes the difference between these two literary rivals but also explains why Mailer has become the voice of his generation while Vidal has become its mocking persona. Even *Myra*, which supposedly reflected the sexual freedom of the sixties, had more in common with the Age of Petronius than it did with the Age of Aquarius.

Vidal's allegiance to a literary past that exists, if anywhere, in the English curriculum of the university, has seriously handicapped him. His vast reading, which must surpass that of any of his American contemporaries, has made his standards rigidly classical. His criticism of novelists like Henry Miller and Saul Bellow rarely concerns their subject matter, but centers on two defects that would also have caught the attention of a Horace or a Longinus: an identification with their characters that is so uncomfortably close that a whine from Herzog is a whine from Bellow; and a style so convoluted that it is downright opaque. Vidal will never accept the argument that tortured, ungrammatical expression would lose its profundity if it were forced to submit to the rules of syntax. Good writing is hard, gemlike prose that softens and grows dull when it becomes confessional.

One speaks wistfully about the Republic of Letters, although Vidal believes every republic sooner or later becomes an empire. Until his death in 1972, Edmund

Wilson was called "our greatest living man of letters." Whenever that accolade was bestowed, the emphasis usually fell on "living," rarely on "man," and never on "letters." The inflection betrayed our fear that he was our only man of letters and that we could prolong his existence by stressing the right word.

Contrary to what the reader may think, I am not going to compare Wilson and Vidal as men of letters. Wilson was unique, Vidal is extraordinary; yet each has earned the title in his own way. Wilson was literally all things to all men. Commencement committees remember him as the ingrate who sent off that unchanging note of regret when he was asked to address the June graduates as they filed into the world. Theologians think of him as the layman who stole the scholars' thunder and clarified the meaning of the Dead Sea scrolls for everyone. History professors who included *To the Finland Station* and *Patriotic Gore* on their reading lists were frequently unaware of *Axel's Castle*, the one book every student of modern literature associates with Edmund Wilson.

If one can assume the Republic of Letters still exists, then Vidal has a place in it—not Edmund Wilson's or Henry James', but his own. Vidal has not published enough verse or short stories to qualify either as a poet or as a short story writer. But he has perfected his own brand of fiction—the literary novel with echoes from Crane, Melville, Twain, Cooper, the eighteenth-century *Bildungsroman*, futuristic fiction, the *Satyricon*, *Nausea*, the New Novel, and even the films of the forties now studied on the campus as "documents of the age." Despite his dislike for the theatre, *Visit to a Small Planet* (which has been anthologized in college readers) and *The Best Man* are extremely well-crafted. Technically, they are melodramas in Lillian Hellman's careful definition of the term—tautly constructed plays relying on conventions (sudden disclosures, chance occurrences) which naturalistic drama avoids but which can be valid if the tricks never become ends in themselves. Some of the television scripts and scenarios were hack work; but the better ones ("Visit to a Small Planet," "Barn Burning," "Turn of the Screw"; *I Accuse, Suddenly Last Summer)* were hardly embarrassing. The essays have made classical rhetoric palatable to a nonclassical age; and even "Edgar Box" once received a favorable notice in the *TLS*.

Before *An Evening with Richard Nixon and . . .* opened, *New York* magazine (May 1, 1972) quoted Vidal as saying he would be moving to Ireland "for good." From West Point to West Cork, so it seems. As an ironist, Gore Vidal would appreciate the fulfillment of one of Gene Vidal's boyhood ambitions:

> I hope one day to stand again
> On a broken rock by the Irish sea,
> And watch the fog banks, full of rain,
> And feel the wind blow free.
> —"Semisonnet" (1942)

Surely a text without need of commentary.

Notes

CHAPTER ONE

[1] "A Note," *Williwaw* (New York: NAL-Signet, 1968), ix.
[2] *Ibid.*, xi.
[3] *After the Lost Generation: A Critical Study of the Writers of Two Wars* (New York: McGraw-Hill, 1951), p. 172.
[4] *In a Yellow Wood* (New York: E. P. Dutton, 1947), p. 91. Subsequent references are to this edition and are given in the text.
[5] *The Diary of Anaïs Nin: Volume Four 1944–1947* (New York: Harcourt Brace Jovanovich, 1971), p. 104; hereafter cited as *"The Diary,"* with page references given in the text.
[6] "The Fourth Diary of Anaïs Nin" (1971), in *Homage to Daniel Shays: Collected Essays 1952–1972* (New York: Random House, 1972), p. 404; hereafter cited in the notes as *"CE."*

CHAPTER TWO

[1] After entering the service in July 1943, Vidal spent the fall term of that year at the Virginia Military Institute in Lexington studying engineering, a field for which he showed little aptitude.
[2] *The City and the Pillar Revised* (New York: E. P. Dutton, 1965), p. 26. Subsequent references are to this edition and are given in the text.
[3] *A Thirsty Evil* (New York: NAL-Signet, 1958), p. 112.
[4] *Two Sisters* (Boston: Little, Brown, 1970), pp. 8–9.

CHAPTER THREE

[1] *After the Lost Generation*, p. 178.

[2] They were divorced in 1941, when the mother of Jacqueline Bouvier Kennedy Onassis became the third Mrs. Auchincloss, and Nina Gore Vidal became Mrs. Robert Olds. The third marriage is not fictionalized in *The Season of Comfort*.

[3] Five of the poems can be found in *Voices* (Summer 1946), pp. 27–29.

[4] *The Season of Comfort* (New York: E. P. Dutton, 1949), p. 34. Subsequent references are to this edition and are given in the text.

[5] *CE*, p. 49.

CHAPTER FOUR

[1] *A Search for the King* (New York: E. P. Dutton, 1950), p. 51. Subsequent references are to this edition and are given in the text.

[2] *Love and Death in the American Novel*, rev. ed. (New York: Delta, 1966), p. 49. Subsequent references are to this edition and are given in the text.

[3] *Dark Green, Bright Red* (New York: NAL-Signet, 1968), p. 23. Subsequent references are to this edition and are given in the text.

CHAPTER FIVE

[1] "Novelists and Critics of the 1940's" (1953), *CE*, p. 7.

[2] *The Judgment of Paris* (Boston: Little, Brown, 1952), p. 3.

CHAPTER SIX

[1] Gerald Clarke, "Petronius Americanus: The Ways of Gore Vidal," *The Atlantic*, March 1972, p. 45.

[2] "Writing Plays for Television" (1956), *CE*, p. 32.

[3] *Theatre Arts*, Dec. 1956, p. 85.

[4] *Visit to a Small Planet and Other Television Plays* (Boston: Little, Brown, 1956), p. 158.

[5] *Daily Variety*, 18 Oct. 1955, p. 19.

CHAPTER SEVEN

[1] *Messiah* (Boston: Little, Brown, 1965), p. 19. Subsequent references are to this edition and are given in the text.
[2] *CE*, p. 70.
[3] *Ibid.*, p. 42.
[4] *Rocking the Boat* (Boston: Little, Brown, 1962), p. 233.
[5] *Voices*, II, no. 3 (Spring 1962), p. 20.
[6] *Julian* (Boston: Little, Brown, 1964), vii-viii. Subsequent references are to this edition and are given in the text.
[7] *CE*, p. 104.

CHAPTER EIGHT

[1] *The Atlantic*, March 1972, p. 50.
[2] The only available text is in *Gore Vidal: Three Plays* (London: William Heinemann, 1962).
[3] "Paranoid Politics" (1967), *CE*, p. 267.
[4] *Washington, D.C.* (Boston: Little, Brown, 1967), p. 321. Subsequent references are to this edition and are given in the text.
[5] *CE*, p. 308.
[6] All quotations are from this edition (New York: Random House, 1972).
[7] During the last week of the run, Vidal himself played Con in the prologue.

CHAPTER NINE

[1] *Myra Breckinridge* (Boston: Little, Brown, 1968), p. 14. Subsequent references are to this edition and are given in the text.
[2] *Screening the Sexes: Homosexuality in the Movies* (New York: Holt, Rinehart and Winston, 1972), p. 201.
[3] *CE*, p. 291.
[4] *Nausea*, trans. Lloyd Alexander (New York: New Directions, 1964), p. 7. Subsequent references are to this edition and are given in the text.
[5] All references in the text are to Arrowsmith's translation (Mentor, 1959).

CHAPTER TEN

[1] *CE*, pp. 234–55.
[2] For the text see Samuel H. Wandell, *Aaron Burr in Literature* (London: Kegan Paul, 1936), pp. 44–47.
[3] *Burr* (New York: Random House, 1973), p. 295. Subsequent references are to this edition and are given in the text.
[4] *CE*, p. 436.

POSTSCRIPT

[1] *Reflections upon a Sinking Ship* (Boston: Little, Brown, 1969), pp. 123–27.

Selected Bibliography

THE WORKS OF GORE VIDAL

NOVELS

Williwaw. New York: E. P. Dutton and Co., 1946.
In a Yellow Wood. New York: E. P. Dutton and Co., 1947.
The City and the Pillar. New York: E. P. Dutton and Co., 1948.
The Season of Comfort. New York: E. P. Dutton and Co., 1949.
A Search for the King. New York: E. P. Dutton and Co., 1950.
Dark Green, Bright Red. New York: E. P. Dutton and Co., 1950. Revised
    edition, 1968.
The Judgment of Paris. New York: E. P. Dutton and Co., 1952. Revised
    edition; Boston: Little, Brown and Co., 1965.
Messiah. New York: E. P. Dutton and Co., 1954. Revised edition;
    Boston: Little, Brown and Co., 1965.
Julian. Boston: Little, Brown and Co., 1964.
The City and the Pillar Revised. New York: E. P. Dutton and Co., 1965.
Washington, D.C. Boston: Little, Brown and Co., 1967.
Myra Breckinridge. Boston: Little, Brown and Co., 1968.
Two Sisters: A Memoir in the Form of a Novel. Boston: Little, Brown and
    Co., 1970.
Burr. New York: Random House, 1973.

"EDGAR BOX" NOVELS

Death in the Fifth Position. New York: E. P. Dutton and Co., 1952.
Death before Bedtime. New York: E. P. Dutton and Co., 1953.
Death Likes It Hot. New York: E. P. Dutton and Co., 1954.

SHORT STORIES

A Thirsty Evil. New York: The Zero Press, 1956.

POETRY

"Five Poems," *Voices* (Summer 1946), 27–29.

PLAYS

Visit to a Small Planet and Other Television Plays. Boston: Little, Brown and Co., 1956.
Visit to a Small Planet. Boston: Little, Brown and Co., 1957.
The Best Man: A Play about Politics. Boston: Little, Brown and Co., 1960.
Gore Vidal: Three Plays. London: William Heinemann, 1962.
Romulus. New York: Grove Press, 1966.
Weekend. New York: Dramatists Play Service, 1968.
An Evening with Richard Nixon. New York: Random House, 1972.

ESSAYS

Rocking the Boat. Boston: Little, Brown and Co., 1962.
Reflections upon a Sinking Ship. Boston: Little, Brown and Co., 1969.
Homage to Daniel Shays: Collected Essays 1952–1972. New York: Random House, 1972.

ANTHOLOGY

Best Television Plays. Edited by Gore Vidal. New York: Ballantine Books, 1956.

JUVENILIA

"To R. K. B.'s Lost Generation," *Phillips Exeter Review*, 9 (Fall 1941), 17.
"Tower of Stone," *Phillips Exeter Review*, 9 (Fall 1941), 24.
"Semisonnet," *Phillips Exeter Review*, 9 (Spring 1942), 14.
"Mostly about Geoffrey," *Phillips Exeter Review*, 10 (Fall 1942), 7–9.
"New Year's Eve," *Phillips Exeter Review*, 10 (Winter 1943), 3–4.
"The Bride Wore a Business Suit," *Phillips Exeter Review*, 10 (Winter 1943), 14–16.
"Union Station," *Phillips Exeter Review*, 10 (Winter 1943), 23.

SECONDARY SOURCES

Aldridge, John W. *After the Lost Generation: A Critical Study of the Writers of Two Wars.* New York: McGraw-Hill, 1951.
Allen, Walter. *The Modern Novel in Britain and the United States.* New York: E. P. Dutton and Co., 1965.

Auchincloss, Eve and Nancy Lynch. "Disturber of the Peace: Gore Vidal," *Mademoiselle*, 58 (September 1961), 132–33, 176–77, 179.

Boyette, Purvis E. "*Myra Breckinridge* and Imitative Form," *Modern Fiction Studies*, 17 (Summer 1971), 229–38.

Clarke, Gerald. "Petronius Americanus: The Ways of Gore Vidal," *The Atlantic*, 229 (March 1972), 44–51.

Fiedler, Leslie. *Love and Death in the American Novel.* 2nd ed. New York: Dell, 1966.

Krim, Seymour. "Reflections on a Ship That's Not Sinking At All," *London Magazine*, 10 (May 1970), 26–43.

Nin, Anaïs. *The Diary of Anaïs Nin: Volume Four 1944–1947.* New York: Harcourt Brace Jovanovich, 1971.

Walter, Eugene. "Conversations with Gore Vidal," *Transatlantic Review* (Summer 1960), 5–17.

White, Ray Lewis. *Gore Vidal.* New York: Twayne, 1968.

Ziolkowski, Theodore. *Fictional Transfigurations of Jesus.* Princeton: Princeton University Press, 1972.